This Book
Presented to

_____

by

_____

on

_____

A MOMENT A DAY

COMPILED BY
MARY BECKWITH & KATHI MILLS

Regal Books

A Division of GL Publications
Ventura, California, U.S.A.

Published by Regal Books
A Division of GL Publications
Ventura, California 93006
Printed in U.S.A.

Library of Congress Cataloging-in-Publication Data

Beckwith, Mary, 1945-
    A moment a day.

    1. Women—Prayer-books and devotions—English. I. Mills, Kathi, 1948-
. II. Title.
BV4844.B39   1988   242'.2'024042   88-4360
ISBN 0-8307-1288-7

4 5 6 7 8 9 10 / 91 90 89

Rights for publishing this book in other languages are contracted by Gospel
Literature International (GLINT) foundation. GLINT also provides technical
help for the adaptation, translation, and publishing of Bible study resources
and books in scores of languages worldwide. For further information, contact
GLINT, Post Office Box 488, Rosemead, California, 91770, U.S.A., or the
publisher.

Dedicated to
Our Mothers, with Love . . .

Remembering Mother

KATHI MILLS

When all the children have grown and gone,
Which memories of Mother will linger on?
Will it be the times she dried their tears,
Held them close and calmed their fears?

The way she always found the time
To read their favorite nursery rhyme,
Over and over, time and again,
Until they knew it, beginning to end.

The sleepless nights with an ailing child—
Mother stayed there all the while,
Ministering love with healing hands,
Spinning tales of faraway lands.

What memories will follow them as they go?
All of these, and more, I know.
But most important, can they say,
"I had a mother who loved to pray."

*Her children arise and call her blessed; her husband
also, and he praises her: "Many women do noble
things, but you surpass them all."*
Proverbs 31:28,29, *NIV*

Contents

Preface

Today's woman is a busy one, whether she stays at home or goes out into the work force. Her time is precious. And yet, with so much "output," she desperately needs some "input"—quick, easy spiritual refills to refresh and renew her.

This book of easy-reading, yet hard-hitting devotions is designed to do just that. Written by women for women, these devotions touch on the various aspects of a busy woman's life—from changing careers to changing diapers. With the addition of poetry and places for prayer requests and praise, this book may sometimes make you laugh—and maybe even cry—but it will definitely help you grow closer to the One who is the Source of all strength and refreshing—Jesus Christ.

Take

MOMENT

DAY

to learn about God . . . .

. . . . Through His Gifts to Us
God Gives Us . . . .

My First Love

BERIT KJOS

As a bridegroom rejoices over his bride, so will your God rejoice over you. Isaiah 62:5, *NIV*

I loved Him the moment we met. He had always loved me. We promised ourselves to one another for all eternity and daily sought new ways to express our love. Our greatest joy was simply to be alone together, sharing our thoughts and dreams. Happily we looked forward to our wedding day!

I had reason to be excited! My Beloved is the most wonderful Bridegroom any bride could imagine. He is kind and understanding beyond comparison. With gentle wisdom, He listens to my every thought, shares each concern and participates in all my activities. His heart is pure and steadfast; nothing can distract Him from being and doing what He knows is right.

My Bridegroom rules the richest, strongest and

most beautiful Kingdom in existence. Therefore, He wields unlimited power to protect, provide and make me truly happy. He is everything I could ever want, for He is altogether perfect and lovely!

But as our engagement period stretched through the years with no set wedding date, I began to lose my initial sense of joy and anticipation of that great day. The wonder and delight of our love-relationship faded, as did the intimacy of our fellowship.

Grieved, my Bridegroom reminded me, "I have loved you with an everlasting love, therefore I have continued to be faithful to you. Will you not be faithful to me?"

Gently, with sadness in His voice, He opened His heart to me. "I miss you. You are so busy these days—so occupied with all the good work of our Kingdom. But you don't have much time for me anymore. Have you lost your first love?"

"Oh, no," I cried. "I love you more than all these other things and people. Somehow, I lost sight of our goal, became distracted and forgot what is most important. I am so sorry! Only you, my Beloved, are my strength, my hope, my joy and my love forever."

Now we continue together—building our love-relationship, as well as the Kingdom that we will share for all eternity. My Beloved is always with me—encouraging, helping and loving me. How precious He is! Together we delight in our intimate fellowship and look forward to that wonderful day when we will meet face to face and our union will be complete. What a day that will be!

Beloved Bridegroom, guard over my heart. Let nothing distract me from the joy of your presence, pre-

cious Jesus, while you continue to show me the glory of our relationship and the wonders of our life together forever. Amen.

Then Came Love
KATHI MILLS

I was lost,
    floating,
        hurting,
looking for an anchor
    to tie on to,
a shoulder to lean on,
a Friend to share my life
    and my secrets with.

I had been disillusioned,
    disappointed,
        disenchanted;
I needed a Rock
to stand strong beneath me,
    always there.
I saw Jesus,
    then came love.

The Sound of God's Presence

MARIAN WIGGINS

I will never leave thee, nor forsake thee.
Hebrews 13:5, *KJV*

Whew! Only one more stop and then I can go home." I gently tossed the sack into the backseat and steered the car toward a neighboring city. As I approached the city, I saw that the outbound traffic was thick, forced into one lane because of road repairs. As I waited for a gap in the traffic so I could turn left, I reflected upon my purchase in that little sack in the backseat. It was a tiny brass bell.

My mom had told me the story. A friend of hers was visiting a teacher at a girls' school. While she was there, a student stood, walked to a side table, picked up a bell, gently rang it, replaced it and returned to her desk. My mom's friend asked what that meant. The teacher replied, "Whenever one of the girls strongly senses the presence of God, she rings the bell to remind others that He is always with us."

I hoped the bell and the accompanying story would bring comfort to a friend of mine who sorely needed to be assured of God's presence in her life.

I was suddenly jarred out of my reverie as I realized my car and I were hurtling through the air at an incredible speed. When we landed, we kept right on going—straight toward the oncoming traffic. My foot on the brake was a futile gesture—there was no stopping the force behind us. My arms ached as I wrenched the wheel to steer clear of traffic. The noise of bursting glass and crushing metal encompassed me.

And then I heard it. The bell.

When the force had spent itself, I turned to see just what had been propelling me forward. My elbow hit the trunk. The backseat was somewhere underneath it. On top of the trunk was a green car. People were screaming. Gasoline was spewing everywhere. Some men pried my door open and pulled me out. I was taken to the hospital for tests. I don't remember much else about all the commotion, for I was awestruck by God's marvelous presence and the overwhelming sense of peace He wove around and through me.

The young driver behind me was unhurt. My car got a new back end—my own back end just got a little bit slower. But what I gained from that experience is the assurance that God indeed is always with me— even in the midst of a crisis.

Lord God, thank you for always being with me. And help me to know when another soul is aching to be encouraged by the promise of your presence. Amen.

. . . Freedom and Abundant Life

Free to Be Me

LUCI SWINDOLL

So Christ has made us free. Now make sure that you stay free and don't get all tied up again in the chains of slavery. Galatians 5:1, *TLB*

Sometimes we're up, at other times we're down, but we need each other. We need others to let us be ourselves—especially those of like faith, on whom we can depend and to whom we should be able to turn for solace. By the same token, we need to allow others to be themselves. Maybe what I'm looking for among a body of Christians doesn't exist. Maybe I'm hoping for too much.

What my spirit reaches out for is that group of people who accept me as I am—warts and all! I'm looking for that support team. I'm looking for that kind of encouragement. I'm looking for a church body that won't always knock me dead with Scripture or spiritualize everything in my life. And tell me, aren't you looking for the same thing?

If the Church has taught me anything, it has—in a strange, unintentional, backhanded sort of way—taught me to value my freedom. Freedom is the natural (and supernatural) by-product of God's grace. It is the gift of God for me to be myself.

Through some bitter lessons I have learned that no church member, no fellow Christian has the right to press me into his or her performance mold. More important, I won't let them do it to me anymore, nor do I want to do it to them.

When I latched onto a knowledge of grace, I also latched onto the liberty that comes with it. I learned how to live abundantly, and that, once and for all, has killed the desire to go back to a narrow, miserly, predictable existence.

I'm free now, and I love it. I'm free from bondage. Free from the law. Free from prejudicial living. Free from wanting to judge others. I've learned the truth, and it has set me free.

Dear Lord, thank you for your love, thank you for your grace, thank you for setting me truly free. Amen.

Adapted from: *The Alchemy of the Heart* by Luci Swindoll, © 1984 by Multnomah Press. Permission granted by the author Luci Swindoll.

Yes, Even a Parking Place

·ELAINE WRIGHT COLVIN

*And we are sure of this, that he will listen to us
whenever we ask him for anything in line with
his will. And if we really know he is listening
when we talk to him and make our requests,
then we can be sure that he will answer us.*
1 John 5:14,15, *TLB*

Oh, no! We're going to have to run for
the ferry again!" I cried. "And, unless we find a parking place in the next minute or two, we're never going
to make it!"

As my college-aged daughter and I struggled
through the downtown Seattle traffic, I thought back
on what a perfect, idyllic place to live Bainbridge
Island had seemed when we first moved there four
years earlier. But that was when Cathy was in high
school and I did my writing and conference planning·
from the little office in our home. Life was certainly
less complicated then!

But now I was working full time to help pay college bills, so all three of us—my husband, my daughter and I—made the daily commute via the Washington State Ferry to Seattle. With a car parked on both sides of the water, praying for parking places had become a daily event.

"I told you we needed to get away from your office sooner," my helpful daughter chided. "You just can't count on finding a parking place within walking distance of the ferry when the waterfront is overrun with summer tourists and conventioners."

"God knew about that last-minute customer I had, and He knows we have to make this ferry in order to get home in time to fix dinner and make it to the church meeting," I assured her.

Then, out loud, I prayed, "Lord, we'll circle this block one more time. Please have someone back out or we're not going to make it."

"Mom, there it is!" Cathy shouted, as we rounded the last corner. "Those people just got in their car. I have to admit—sometimes you have a lot more faith than I do. Who'd think God would be interested in whether or not we find a parking place?"

"But that's the exciting part of it," I explained. "God *is* interested in every part of our lives—even schedules and parking places. Now, let's run for it!"

Hurriedly, we locked the car, grabbed our bags and dashed across the street. By now, we were huffing and puffing as we ran up the escalator, threw our tickets on the counter and sprinted down the gangplank. We were just stepping onto the ferry when the *too-late* whistle blew.

Dropping into the nearest empty seats, Cathy and I looked at each other and grinned. "Thank you, God," I murmured. "You came through for us again!

25

But, next time, could you manage to give us a minute or two to spare?"

Lord, thank you for being interested in the seemingly insignificant details of my life. Help me to rejoice in any kind of day you give me. Amen.

The Sea of Life
DIANTHA AIN

Bless me, Lord,
    With the strength of the tide,
So my every move
    Will have you as a guide.
Let me rise to meet
    Each adversity,
While I staunchly cling
    To my faith in Thee.

... Miracles Great and Small

Our Miracle Van

INGRID SHELTON

Jesus did many other things as well. If every one of them were written down, I suppose that even the whole world would not have room for the books that would be written.
John 21:25, *NIV*

We need a miracle," I told my friend Jan. "Our VW van is far too old to take us across the United States, and we've had a lot of problems with it lately. We're looking for a good used one, but they're rare. The ones we found are far too expensive."

"Let's pray about it," Jan suggested. "God has promised to answer prayer, and miracles still happen."

And that's what we did. Week after week, we prayed, expecting a miracle. Two months later, we were still praying for our *miracle van*. My faith began to weaken. Did miracles really still happen today, I wondered. Did I have the right to expect one?

As I was packing our old van for the trip across the country, my husband said, "We'll just dump it if the motor or transmission goes. It's not worth much anyway. We can always rent a car or take a bus home."

I was disappointed that our miracle van hadn't materialized. Yet, I was eager to go on our family vacation. In the excitement and enjoyment of our trip, I completely forgot about the condition of our old van. It wasn't until we returned home that I realized God had indeed granted us a miracle van. Apart from a flat tire, we'd had no car trouble at all.

Thanking God for giving us a safe and good trip, I realized that miracles are a part of life. They come in various forms and in unexpected ways. Not only did the Lord keep our van from breaking down, but He allowed us to experience other miracles on our trip: good health, the kindness of our hosts, refreshing and sound sleep in various strange places, the grandeur of Old Faithful at Yellowstone Park, the beauty and uniqueness of the New England states.

God is constantly favoring us with miracles, which, for us as Christians, began with the new birth—salvation—the greatest miracle of all.

Dear Lord, thank you for the miracle of your love. Help me to recognize your miraculous doings in every circumstance of my life. Amen.

Language of Love

MARY LOU CARNEY

Peace I leave with you, my peace I give unto you: not as the world giveth, give I unto you. Let not your heart be troubled, neither let it be afraid. John 14:27, *KJV*

The story is told of Bozo, the circus elephant, who was scheduled for execution in the center ring. It seems that Bozo had changed from a well-behaved performer to a vicious animal, trying three times to kill his trainer.

Rifles were stacked along the side of the ring. Bozo trudged in a circle inside the steel cage, raising his trunk to trumpet his rage. But just as the ringmaster lifted his arm to give the fatal signal, a small man stepped forward.

"Let me in the cage," he pleaded. "In two minutes I will show you that Bozo is not a bad elephant." Surprised, but anxious to salvage his investment if possible, the ringmaster opened the cage, and the stranger stepped inside.

Bozo whirled around and glared through blood-shot eyes at the intruder. Softly, the man began to speak. Bozo stopped pacing and listened. His massive body quivered into relaxation. A small, childlike cry echoed from his huge trunk. Astonished, the crowd broke into applause.

That man was Rudyard Kipling. He had spoken to the elephant in Hindustani, knowing that the Indian beast was simply homesick. Kipling's words had made Bozo feel at peace again.

Sometimes we Christians, too, become homesick. Surrounded by the wickedness and misery of this world, we are tempted to despondency. We long for our heavenly home. That's when we need to hear again Christ's promise of peace, a promise spoken in the language of divine love.

We must live our lives in the world, Father, but let us rest in your peace. Amen.

... His Wisdom

A Complete Puzzle

DAISY HEPBURN

Thank you for making me so wonderfully complex! It is amazing to think about.
Psalm 139:14, *TLB*

It was evident that this was the very first time she had been able to gather enough courage to give her testimony. Finding the desire in her heart was not a surprise, but to get the words past her throat where they had been stuck for weeks—and into the big world of *risk*—was quite another thing.

She quivered and quaked, stuttered and shook, and then: "Be-before I c-came to know Jesus Christ, my l-l-life was l-like a p-p-puzzle with one p-piece m-m-missing." She caught her breath, and her statement of faith was formed, confident and sure: "Now that I know Christ as my Savior, my life is a complete puzzle!"

A round of joyful applause confused her, but those of us who had been walking for some time with the Lord suddenly found our hearts warmed as we reflected on even the simple events and experiences of the day.

Be it an out-of-balance checking account; a dress pattern that calls for more fabric than we purchased; two commitments and a phone call for the same time slot—our daily lives are often puzzling. How can we know the Lord's special will for a particular situation? Should I lead the Sunday School class, or start a neighborhood Bible study group? Who will care for my children if this illness is more serious than it appears?

God has promised His wisdom. The only condition attached is that I really believe the decisions I make about my time, money, abilities and are authored by the Holy Spirit in response to my request for His direction. If I am indecisive and wavering, I will be unstable in all my ways (see Jas. 1:8). How marvelous to know that He will help me put all the pieces of my life together in one complete puzzle!

Help me today, Lord, to thank you for making me so wonderfully complex. Then teach me to depend on your wisdom. Amen.

Claiming His Promises

DIANE JUSTUS

It should be that of your inner self, the unfading beauty of a gentle and quiet spirit, which is of great worth in God's sight.
1 Peter 3:4, NIV

Screaming shrilly at my son to stop picking on his brother, I sat down heavily in a chair. Head pounding, back aching, I started to cry. "Where are you, God? You promised peace and joy, and here I am, yelling at the boys—again. I know you can't lie, so what's wrong?"

As I closed my eyes and cried out to Jesus, His peace began to filter through my throbbing brain like summer rain on a baked field. Sighing deeply, I stretched my cramped legs and snuggled back into the chair. God was still with me; He had not given up on me in spite of my continual outbursts. Yet where was the power to overcome my anger?

Slowly I began to understand that the promises of God are apprehended by faith—they are not automatically dumped on us when we become Christians. There are powerful promises in God's Word, which meet every need and situation in the life of the believer. God's mighty resurrection power is unleashed to transform us into the image of Christ, as His Word is understood and appropriated by faith.

As God's peace began to lighten my load of anger and guilt, I picked up my Bible and turned to 1 Peter 3:4, where I read about the beauty of a gentle and quiet spirit being of great worth in God's sight. Anything of great worth in God's sight I wanted, and I definitely was not of a gentle and a quiet spirit! I knew from this Scripture that God wanted me to be peaceful and gentle and I understood that His Word would empower me to become what He wanted, so I claimed that verse as God's promise to me.

I continue to struggle often with my temper, but every time it threatens to overwhelm me, I quote this verse over and over again until it accomplishes its powerful work deep within the recesses of my being.

Last week a friend said, "Do you know what I admire most about you? Your gentle, quiet spirit." I laughed, knowing that God's resurrection power had done it again! He had transformed another part of me into His image.

Dear Jesus, thank you for making your resurrection power available to us so that we are not left to our own weaknesses. Thanks for changing us through the strength of your Word. Amen.

34

. . . Patience for All Things

I Want It Now!

DIANTHA AIN

Let patience have her perfect work.
James 1:4, *KJV*

Dear God, give me patience . . . and give
it to me right now!"

When my husband says that at the perfect
moment in a social situation, he nearly always
receives a big laugh. But how many times in my life
have I uttered that very prayer? The desire for instant
gratification comes out of the womb with us, and
none of us is eager to part with it.

Learning to be patient was never high on my list of
priorities until I had a baby of my own, who taught
me some hard lessons about patience. Yet with all my
years of practice, being patient with a child successfully did not help me to accomplish the same miracle
at an adult level.

But being a patient in a hospital for a couple of

35

weeks gave me a powerful advantage. I wouldn't be surprised to discover that's where the terminology—*patient, patience*—originated. Or, maybe it was in the doctor's waiting room. I figure they must feel obligated to prepare us a little, just in case we have to go to the hospital.

The task of caring for a loved one who is seriously ill somehow makes the whole process more palatable. My various hospital stays taught me how to cope with pain and depression, which I knew could distort even the sunniest disposition.

All these experiences formed a mighty reservoir of insight for me to draw upon. My pump is that same little prayer, "Dear God, give me patience." And He does. Concentrating on Him is the most expedient way I know to find the strength to do what I need to do—with patience.

It has even helped me over the hardest hurdle of all—being patient with myself.

Let me always strive to do your will, Dear God, with patience, fortitude and a loving heart. Amen.

The Winters of Life

PEG RANKIN

Be still, and know that I am God.
Psalm 46:10, *KJV*

I was brought up on a farm in southern New Jersey. For me the winter season was a very special time. Daddy didn't work as hard as he did the rest of the year. In fact, there were periods of time when he didn't work at all—so far as I could tell. He just sat by the fire and held me close. Oh, how I treasured those intimate moments!

I treasure the winters in my spiritual life, too— those times when the demands to be active are not as heavy as usual. How good it is to come apart from the frantic pace of life, to feel the warmth of my Father's love in a refreshing way.

Sometimes, when I am resting in His arms, He

speaks directly to my heart. "My child, I love you. I *love* you," He emphasizes. "Do you mind if I hold you tightly for just a moment? You need to calm down. You've been running."

As I snuggle closer to Him, He gently probes, "Why do you think you are pleasing me only when you are actively accomplishing something for me? Don't you know I am much more interested in what you are *becoming* than in what you are *doing* for the advancement of my kingdom? Learn what it means to be still. Just *be still*—and get to know me. I am your Protector, your Provider, your Comforter and your Healer. And, my child, I dearly love you. Understand that."

Lord, I have been running. I confess it. Now calm me. Still my soul and hold me close—so close I can feel the heartbeat of your love and hear you whisper precious promises of peace in my ear. I want to get to know you. I want to make the most of the winters of my life. In Jesus' name, Amen.

. . . Renewed Hope

From Darkness to Light

CHRISTINE RICH

*This is the message we have heard from him
and declare to you: God is light; in him there is
no darkness at all.* 1 John 1:5, *NIV*

The sun was already warm on my skin
as we trudged out to the hospital parking lot that
spring morning. I jerked my head upward toward the
blazing yellow ball and cried, "How can you shine so
brightly when my son's light has just burned out?"

The darkness of death shrouded me as I began the
long and treacherous journey through the grief process. I was unprepared and unskilled at sorrow.
Every new phase crashed in upon me with feelings of
uncertainty and despair. The God I loved and trusted
had disappeared and left me forsaken. My faith,
which had been the solid base of my life, exploded
into millions of tiny pieces. I had no reason to live on.

Three weeks after Bobby's death, the need to write carved its way into my daily, minute-by-minute struggle with grief. Becoming a writer had not been a childhood dream of mine but, in the midst of this tragedy, the need to put my innermost thoughts on paper burned within my soul.

Writing became as vital for life as breathing. In the wee hours of the morning, when nightmares of Bobby's accident ran through my mind in living color, I stumbled out to the kitchen table with paper and pen in hand. Page after page, my anger and fears surfaced in black and white. The journal became my confidant—a secret friend who never tired of my cries of heartache and emptiness.

I blundered down the road of grief all alone—or so I thought. My writings, however, revealed otherwise. Scattered among the debris of my sorrow, some beauty had seeped in. The handiwork of God sparkled like a precious gem in a cold, dark cave. I had written about hearing the melodic song of a bird one morning, and seeing the serenity of horses grazing in a meadow sprinkled with morning dew.

The truth ripped through me—God hadn't forsaken me! He had been my confidant all along! He used my journal as a guide to lead me out of darkness into the brightness of His world outside.

Father, without you, I never would have turned my despair into hope. Thank you! Amen.

... A Hiding Place

When Things Go Wrong

MARTHA BOLTON

God is our refuge and strength, a very present help in trouble. Psalm 46:1, *KJV*

Lord, help me today when things go wrong.

When I get that shopping cart with only three wheels and they're all going in different directions, help me to know my strength comes from you.

Be with me as I drop off my children at soccer practice, Little League, piano lessons, the library, a birthday party and Girl Scouts. Help me to remember to be at the right place at the right time to pick up the right kid.

And today, should my washing machine break down, my dishwasher overflow and my refrigerator decide to start making slushes out of my cartons of milk, help me to be thankful that they did make it a full week beyond their warranty expiration dates.

And, Lord, when dinner burns, and the dog tracks in mud on my newly waxed floors, grant me patience as I toss them both out.

Comfort me when I realize I missed that important appointment at two o'clock because that door-to-door salesman who came at one wouldn't let me get a word in edgewise until three-thirty.

And when the bottom falls out of my trash bag, help me to look on the bright side. All those empty cereal boxes lying there and those opened cans rolling around on the floor mean I haven't had to go hungry.

And if my mailman's late, my carpool's early, and those dinner guests I forgot about inviting arrive on time, let me rest in your peace.

Finally, Lord, when I dash to take the kids to school in my robe and curlers, and run out of gas at the front entrance, let me hide in your love.

. . . For, Lord, when things go wrong, I need to remember that you have a way of making everything right again. Amen.

... Bright Hope for Tomorrow

Promises in the Rain

SHARON MAHOE

And we know that all things work together for good to them that love God, to them who are the called according to his purpose.
Romans 8:28, *KJV*

It was not a very good year. In fact, it had not been a very good year for what seemed like a very long time. But, in my experience of crying and reaching out to God, as well as to others, I was finding a deeper understanding of what God means when He says, "I will never leave thee, nor forsake thee" (Heb. 13:5, *KJV*).

It is always painful to go through the deeps, and mine seemed to be lasting longer than necessary! My fierce independence and self-sufficiency were being melted down to create a more beautiful dependence on God for His direction in my life. I felt as though I were a grapevine waiting for the owner of the vineyard to sweep down the row one more time and hack away at my branches, pruning and pruning until it hurt so much I wanted to cry: Enough already! Go on to someone else!

And then, one drizzly, blustery afternoon, while driving down the California coast from Santa Barbara, reflecting on the painful months behind me and what I had learned through it all, I came face-to-face with a stunning double rainbow. I thrilled to the colors sifting in and out of the clouds, and I talked to God about my feelings. I told Him I was glad I had learned so much about His faithfulness and love for me, and I did not ever wish to be off track in my relationship with Him again. And when I made mistakes, as I knew I would, I asked Him to please work it all out for the best and help me accept and understand what I should learn from the experience.

As the car curved around the freeway ramp, I was still thinking and praying. Suddenly the rain ceased. A car passed me, splashing up the puddles. The license plate on the back caught my attention: *8 ROM 28*. There was God's answer to my prayer, almost before I had prayed it. Never before had I seen that car. It rounded the corner, out of my sight. My eyes filled with tears. God talked to me through a license plate. He reminded me that because I am His child, all things would work out for the best, no matter how hurtful, how puzzling they seemed to be at the time.

Thank you, Lord, that I can depend on you to work out the details of my life. Amen.

... Renewed Trust

But I Don't Want to Go!

MARIETTA GRAMCKOW

Trust in the Lord with all thine heart; and lean not unto thine own understanding. In all thy ways acknowledge him, and he shall direct thy paths. Proverbs 3:5,6 *KJV*

But I don't want to go, Grandma! Please let me stay here with you!" These words are stated emphatically—and often—by my young grandson almost everytime someone suggests going anywhere. Because he comes to stay at our house when my son and daughter-in-law are at work, he spends a lot of time with me. He's used to being here with me; he's comfortable here; he does not like change.

How well I can relate to that! I remember when my husband said he wanted to move from Southern California to the state of Washington when we retired. The very thought depressed me! How many times I protested, "But I don't want to go! This is my home. All my friends are here, and my church, and . . . "

But the more I fought it, the more God assured me He was in control, that if I trusted Him He would take care of friends, church—everything. Now, 15 years after that much-dreaded move, I see how much I would have missed if I'd dug in my heels and refused to go. Besides a wonderful church home and countless friends, God has blessed me with a lovely daughter-in-law (whom my son never would have met in California) and a darling grandson who just wants to stay at home with his grandma! God's ways are definitely higher and greater than ours.

Dear Lord, forgive me for the times I haven't trusted you as I should. Help me to accept more graciously and willingly your plans for my life. Amen.

Take a moment to praise God and list blessings you've received from trusting Him:

Custom-Made Problems

ETHEL BARRETT

The brother in humble circumstances ought to take pride in his high position. But the one who is rich should take pride in his low position, because he will pass away like a wild flower. James 1:9,10, NIV

Are you poor? Are you lacking in money, in talent, in looks, in opportunities, in "the breaks"? Rejoice! You are of great worth to God. You are of worth in the church, in the world. You are rich—rich! You are a child of the *King. God* is your Father. Rejoice in the things you *cannot lose.*

Are you rich? Money can be lost, talent can be snatched away, looks can fade, circumstances can change for the worse. Happy are you if you are aware of this. Rejoice in the things you *cannot lose.*

In between these two extremes lies every conceivable combination of circumstances, gifts, talents, "breaks." And no matter where you are on the scale, you will have problems, and they are custom-made for you.

You are uniquely you; there is nobody else who has ever been born who is quite like you. And the testings God sends into your life are to meet your needs, show you your weaknesses, develop your character. To give a problem a name (trouble in a marriage, handicap, disease, poverty, betrayal, gossip mongers, etc.) and pop it into a category and then go down in fear under its onslaught is to stumble over semantics; you are afraid of words. And the words might not mean exactly the same things in your case as they do in other cases, for even if the circumstances seem the same, you are different.

So in the last analysis, it's just you and your problem—and God.

Dear Lord, help us to rejoice in whatever situation you've placed us, and to see our custom-made problems as a means of growth. Amen.

Adapted from *Will the Real Phony Please Stand Up?* by Ethel Barrett. © Copyright 1969, 1984 by Regal Books, Ventura, California 93006. Used by permission.

The Challenge of Silence

PEG RANKIN

They that wait upon the Lord shall renew their strength; they shall mount up with wings as eagles; they shall run, and not be weary; and they shall walk, and not faint.
Isaiah 40:31, *KJV*

Have you ever had the experience of riding in a car with someone you love and suddenly realizing you have traveled several miles without a word passing between you? Were you uncomfortable? Probably not if you felt close to and unthreatened by the one sitting next to you.

Quiet tongues do not necessarily mean quiet minds. We know that. In fact, quite the opposite usually proves true. Contemplation can give birth to some very exciting plans.

If, however, the one beside us is a stranger, then silence can be very uncomfortable indeed. In fact, we make every effort to keep the conversation going, even to the point of talking trivia.

So it is with our relationship with God. The better we know Him, the more at ease we are with His silence. We have learned that silence does not mean unconcern, but rather the birth of some very great plans. At those times when there seems to be little indication of divine intervention on earth, some very exciting things may be in the works of heaven.

For example, in the interim between the almost continuous interaction of God and man in the Old Testament and the birth of Christ at the beginning of the New Testament, there was a period of silence that lasted 400 years. Then, between the exciting birth announcement of the angels and the start of the non-stop ministry of Jesus, there was another period of quiet preparation that lasted 30 years.

Following the furor surrounding Jesus' trial and eventual crucifixion, there was yet another period of silence. True, it lasted only one day, but to the disciples who didn't understand, it must have seemed like an eternity. Then Jesus appeared, this time in Resurrection power! Silence had given birth to expression; waiting, to exciting revelation.

Oh, Lord, teach me to wait. Assure me that when you appear to be least active in my life, you are actually waiting for the right time to become most active. I am ready for some of that activity, Lord. Bless me. In Jesus' name, Amen.

Another Move

ELAINE WRIGHT COLVIN

For promotion and power come from nowhere on earth, but only from God. He promotes one and deposes another. Psalm 75:6,7, *TLB*

My husband popped through the front door of our Boise home calling, "Hi, honey, how was your day?"

An ominous feeling crept over me. Was it the tone of his voice? An unusual bounce to his usually fast-paced walk? Something was definitely different. "Oh, it was all right," I answered guardedly. "How about yours?"

"Super! You know, I told the Lord I was willing to live right here for the rest of my life if He wanted us to. But . . . well, today I got a promotion, and we're moving to Montana!"

My mouth dropped open. The room whirled. I managed a weak, "Oh? When?" as my world crashed down around me. This time I was sure God must not

51

know what He was doing. Wasn't it enough that we had already moved back and forth across the United States six times in the past dozen years?

We managed to get through dinner, and I left early for my church discipleship class. I knew I needed time alone with God before I broke the news to my friends.

Slipping into the prayer chapel, I glanced around, thankful it was empty at this early hour. "Okay, God, you've really gone and done it this time! Do you know how hard it is to sell a house during the Christmas holidays? Not to mention the mess of packing and driving north in the dead of winter! What about pulling Cathy out of school, and leaving my Christian writers' club?"

My ranting and raving finally subsided and, while the tears fell softly on my Bible, I prayed. "Now, it's your turn, God. Please show me a promise to claim in your Word so that I know this move is really going to be all right for all of us."

As I leafed through the pages of my Bible, His answer came through loud and clear. *I am the Lord your God, who teaches you what is best for you, who directs you in the way you should go* (Isa. 48:17, *NIV*).

Father, help me to walk in the faith that you know what is best for me at all times. Amen.

. . . The Desires of Our Heart

His Perfect Timing

KATHI MILLS

Delight yourself in the Lord and he will give you the desires of your heart. Psalm 37:4, *NIV*

Growing up in a house full of brothers (and all their seemingly dirty, noisy, obnoxious friends), I was envious of my girlfriends who had sisters—sisters to share rooms and secrets and late-night giggles with. Then, as I grew older and began to appreciate the special closeness I shared with my mother, I gave up on the idea of a sister and began to look forward to the relationships I would someday share with my own daughters.

But that didn't happen. Instead, God blessed me with three wonderful sons—none of whom I would trade for a thousand daughters. My relationship with my mother is better than ever, and I have a dear mother-in-law who has become a second mother to me, as well. On top of all that, my youngest brother married just the lady I would have picked out for my very own sister had I been given the chance.

So how could I ever again complain or feel cheated because I didn't have a daughter? I decided long ago that God, in His infinite wisdom and perfect plan for my life, had more than made up for not giving me the daughters I had wished and prayed for.

But God is so good—and His timing so perfect! With my fortieth birthday just around the corner (and all thoughts of ever having a daughter long forgotten) my 19-year-old son, Michael, called to say he was getting married.

Oh, Lord, I cried silently, trying to hide my fears while offering my congratulations, *they're so young! How will they ever survive the pressures and strains of marriage in a world that scorns commitment? What if it all falls apart and they are both terribly hurt? What if...*

"Trust me," God seemed to whisper. "This is all a part of my plan—and an answer to your prayers."

Michael and Christy have been married several months now, and the other day I received a card in the mail that read "For You on Mother-in-Law's Day" (I hadn't even realized there was such a thing!). On the inside, it was addressed to "Mom," and signed with love.

As I gently set the card on the file cabinet next to Christy's picture in my office, I blinked back the tears and thanked God for giving me the desire of my heart. I finally had my daughter.

Father, thank you that your timing is always right.

And thank you for the promise that, when we delight
ourselves in you, you give us the desires of our
hearts. Amen.

Testimony
MARILYN HOCHHEISER

Because you said
when you were spit upon,
scorned, hung on a tree,
"Father, forgive them;
for they know not what they do,"
my eyes were opened
that I could recognize you.

Because you stood
in the gap,
taking my place
at the whipping post,
sorrowing for my peace,
I was healed, made whole
through your wounded flesh, and grief.

Because you were
lifted high upon the cross,
giving me the victory
through your blood and name,
defeating Satan's lies,
I can rejoice for in you, Jesus,
there is life.

His Magnificent Stained Glass Window

SUSAN F. TITUS

All of you together are the one body of Christ and each one of you is a separate and necessary part of it. 1 Corinthians 12:27, *TLB*

The vase slipped from my hands and crashed on the kitchen floor. The cut roses lay neatly on the counter, but the crystal jar I had intended for their use was shattered. I could never mend it.

Most of us experience a time when our lives are splintered like that vase. A number of women lose a spouse or a child. Others suffer from illnesses or severe personal problems.

How do we react in a time of crisis? A few do nothing because the problems overwhelm them. Other women allow God to use those opportunities to strengthen their faith and shape them in His image.

God gives us the choice. We can accept God's help, or we can remain on the ground—shattered, bored, hopeless, questioning, rationalizing. The decision is ours.

God created each woman to be unique. He wants us to allow Him to pick up the fractured slivers representing our lives. He will mend and reshape them, once again making us whole.

The stained glass windows of magnificent cathedrals are examples of what can be done with boxes of broken glass. If we allow Him, God will use us to form the pieces of His *magnificent stained glass window*. He places each fragment of glass in the perfect place He has chosen.

Each segment of glass depends on every other part for the picture to be complete, but it takes God to hold us together.

Next time you have a chance, observe a stained glass window. Watch the sun piercing through each unique pane of glass. Then notice how many shapes and sizes are necessary to form the whole.

Dear Lord, please use the difficult circumstances that enter my life to strengthen me. Shape me to be whom and what you desire. Amen.

Take
A
MOMENT
A
DAY
to learn about God . . .

. . . Through Our Gifts to Him
We Give Him . . .

. . . Our Faith and Trust

A Walk in the Fog

BERYL HENNE

For we walk by faith, not by sight.
2 Corinthians 5:7, *KJV*

A brisk walk in the early morning—how I love it! Not only does it wake me up and clear my head, but it's a wonderful time to hold an uninterrupted conversation with the Lord. My favorite spot is along a dike, away from traffic and other distracting noises.

One fall morning, I found myself in the midst of a thick cloud of fog. I had never walked in fog before, so I found it interesting to be unable to see any of my usual landmarks. I could see only about five feet in any direction around me. But the more I walked, the more I saw—within my five-foot radius. I noticed also that, even though my hair was getting wet and the moisture was standing in droplets on my jacket, the ground was dry.

The parallels were obvious to me that morning. No matter how much *rain* comes into my life, my feet are on dry ground. My footing is sure when I trust Jesus Christ with every detail. And when I am trusting, it doesn't matter how far ahead I can see. If I keep on taking the few steps that are clear to me, the next steps become visible in the process. On the other hand, if I don't take any steps because I can't see far ahead, I will never get anywhere.

The Christian life is like my walk in the fog—we don't see very far at any given time. We must take the steps we know, and believe God for the rest. At the end of the road, we will look back and praise God for the way He chose to lead us. That is what faith is all about.

Thank you, Father, for the gift of faith, which you have given to every believer. May I be a faithful walker today. Amen.

... Our Lives to Use

Reflections

SHARON MAHOE

*Now we see but a poor reflection as in a
mirror.* 1 Corinthians 13:12, *NIV*

T he mirror was at least 100 years old.
Its curves bubbled out of the top and down each side
to curl in graceful repose on its shoulders. It had
been painted a Wedgewood blue, underneath which
was hidden a lovely oak grain waiting to be given a
coat of stain and some varnish to show off the simple,
sloping curves.

Frances wanted me to have it. To remember her
always, she said. I was thrilled. A friend restored its
finish to a beautiful brown and designed a backing
that would hold my gift safely against the wall above
the sofa. The sofa was an old loveseat, upholstered in
flowered fabric. It could open out at each end to make
into a small bed. I would often sit across the room
and look at the mirror and the reflected parts of my
living room in its silvery haze.

What a story it could tell! Of newlyweds. A mother and her babies, sitting in the chair before the fire. Or a pair of grandparents, waiting for the children to arrive for the holidays.

Months passed. The mirror was already part of my own memories. The flicker of the candles sitting on the piano and the warm shine of polished brass caught the light and created another imaginary, secret room to which I would often retreat.

Then one day Frances called. "I'd like the mirror back," she said. My heart slowed. But why? "I've the perfect place for it after all and, besides, I never felt I really gave it to you anyway." My eyes stung with tears as I packed it lovingly and returned it, so very reluctantly, to my friend's home.

No, this story never happened. Frances did not call and ask me to return the mirror. I still have it, and it warms my heart every time I remember the friend who gave it to me to enjoy.

But years ago, I gave the Lord my life, to use and enjoy. And then, years later, I took it back to do with what I wanted. I'm sure His heart slowed, also, as He waited for me to learn what giving a gift really means, and for me to offer myself back to Him.

Have we truly given our lives to God? Or have we broken His heart by taking them back?

Lord Jesus, thank you for giving me such a wonderful gift, one that I may keep—eternal salvation. I renew my promise to give you my life to use for your glory. Amen.

... Our Sense of Humor

No Time for Camels

KATHI MILLS

He will yet fill your mouth with laughter.
Job 8:21, *NIV*

It was the morning of back-to-school night at my son's elementary school, and since I was PTA president, it was up to me to see that everything ran smoothly. I got up at five, hoping to get my housework done early. By the time I hurried my son off to school, I decided to start some laundry before leaving for work.

Realizing it was time for one of my favorite radio programs, I flipped the switch just as the speaker was telling how Abraham had sent his servant to get a wife for Abraham's son Isaac. When the servant arrived at his destination, it was "the time the women go out to draw water" (Gen. 24:11, *NIV*). He went on to explain how Rebekeh drew water for Abraham's servant, and then for all ten of his camels as well. Then he added, "Of course, that was in the days before automatic washers and dryers or microwave ovens. Let me tell you, in those days women really worked!"

Gasping, I stared at the radio in disbelief. "Oh yeah?" I hollered, snatching my pile of perma-press from the floor. "Well, let me tell you something!" I was still muttering when I stormed out of the house 15 minutes later.

Shortly after noon, I left work, still upset, and spent the early part of the afternoon preparing things at the school. By the time I finished that, my son was home, needing help with his homework, as well as transportation to and from soccer practice. Somewhere in between all that I got dinner ready (defiantly using my microwave), and then ran out the door to head back to the school. Balancing a cash box, several ledger sheets, my purse and three binders, I fumbled with my keys, trying to unlock the car door. Suddenly everything slipped and crashed to the ground, the heavy cash box landing on my foot.

As I stood there, my foot screaming in pain, a tiny bubble of laughter began rolling around in my chest. A silly grin tugged at the corners of my mouth, and soon I was chuckling softly. "Oh, Lord, how ridiculous I am! How could I have let one remark, which had nothing to do with me, ruin my walk with you today? Forgive me, Lord, and thank you for the gift of laughter!"

Midway through back-to-school night, a woman came up to me and shook her head. "How in the world do you do it? I mean, you're so organized! Have you ever considered doing workshops on how to manage your time?"

I swallowed a giggle and tried to look serious. "No. And I don't water camels, either."

Lord, help me to remember to appreciate—and spread—your gift of laughter. Amen.

———————

Take a moment to praise God and list some humorous times in your life:

. . . Our Prayers

The Only Rule
of Prayer Is Pray

FAY ANGUS

Lord, teach us to pray. Luke 11:1, *NASB*

Without circumventing scriptural direc-
tionals, encouragements and admonitions (and there
are many), the bottom line of prayer is to pray. When
we do, the power of heaven picks up momentum to
change our lives.

Much as we try to put Him there, God is not on
trial; the good news is that neither is man. Jesus
Christ stood in the docket on our behalf.

If the answers to our prayers depended upon our
worth, they would never be answered—they would
never even be heard. Through the righteousness of
Christ, they are.

We tend to stroke prayer like a lucky rabbit's foot,

and seek God's fleece rather than His face.

We try to manipulate His will to ours and sometimes call it faith. We push forward in the arrogance of our own stoic determination, limited by our finite vision, rather than pull back in the simple trust of His infinite plan.

We expect Him to change the sovereignty of His omnipotent heart, instead of humbly asking Him to give us a heart willing to be changed.

"Be still, and know that I am God," (Ps. 46:10, *KJV*) means, "Relax, let God be God."

I thank God for the prayers He has answered the way I prayed that He would.

I thank Him, somewhat shamefully, for the prayers I prayed and then forgot all about; but He didn't, and in His lovingkindness He answered them anyway.

I also thank God for the prayers He didn't answer the way I prayed He would. I shudder to think of how some things in my life may have turned out if He had!

, In the mystery of His timing, in the confusion where I do not understand—God is God. I will not diagnose Him, I will not analyze Him. I will obey Him, I will adore Him, and I will continue to lay my life before Him.

Dear heavenly Father, thank you for prayer, thank you for your sovereignty, thank you for your infinite love. Amen.

Adapted from *How to Do Everything Right and Live to Regret It* by Fay Angus. © Copyright 1983 by Fay Angus. Published by Harper & Row, San Francisco, CA. Used by permission.

Stepping Out in Ministry

MARIETTA GRAMCKOW

I can do all things through Christ which strengtheneth me. Philippians 4:13 KJV

My writing in the past has consisted of an extensive letter-writing ministry. But letters are one thing; writing for publication is quite another. "Lord," I prayed, "you know I've never done anything quite like this before. But if you want me to, I'm going to need your help!"

As my deadline drew near, the Lord reminded me of the parable of the talents, as well as His commandment to go forth and preach the gospel to every creature. When I concentrated on those thoughts, I realized that He has given to each of us at least one talent. If we are afraid to use it, if we keep it hidden, it will not gain a thing. It will become corrupt and useless.

Still, I was unable to get anything on paper. And then I remembered that God does not ask us to do what He has not given us the ability to do. He asks only that we be faithful in yielding to His power to use the talent He has given us. In whatever way He provides, we are to tell others the good news.

I rolled the paper into the typewriter, thanking and praising Him for His gifts and promises.

Father, I thank you for your faithfulness. Help me to be faithful to you. Amen.

———

Take a moment to praise God and list the talents He has given you:

More Than a Servant

BARBARA COOK

I no longer call you servants, because a servant does not know his master's business. Instead, I have called you friends, for everything that I have learned from my Father I have made known to you. John 15:15, *NIV*

It wasn't my birthday. It wasn't an anniversary, either. But I received a card that made my day. On the front, it said: *You've been more than a parent . . . you've been my friend.* Inside was a note saying: *Dear Mom, Thanks for our great friendship. Lots of love for you always, Christi.*

Christi is 21, out of college, employed in a career she loves. She has a great marriage and is busy in her church. She doesn't need much mothering anymore. And I'm glad—because it's so good to have her for a friend.

This transition from mother/child relationship to adult friendship came somewhere during Christi's teen years, and was complete by the time she was married. We do a lot of fun things together just because we enjoy each other. When she was a baby, I hadn't even a glimpse of the kind of wonderfully satisfying relationship she would bring into my life.

Back in those years, there seemed to be a lot of Christian teaching about Lordship. Knowing Jesus as Savior wasn't enough, it was emphasized. It was necessary to make Him Lord and Master, as well. Like other Bible teachers, I did my share of preaching about the necessity of obeying God, serving Him in every daily act, doing His will at all times. Many of the sermons went so far as to compare myself to a slave (a love-slave, of course, as Paul described himself, but a slave nevertheless, with no rights or privileges of my own—no desires, dreams, goals, creativity, no pleasures except that of serving the Master).

In our seriousness about Lordship, we almost overlooked the conversation Jesus had with His disciples, explaining the relationship He really wanted with them. A slave asks no questions, needs no understanding from the master, doesn't even need to think. A slave simply follows orders. It would be out of line, even rebellious, for a slave to ask questions about the larger picture. "How do I fit into the scheme of things? What are you trying to accomplish? What is the work we are doing?"

"A servant does not know his master's business," Jesus said in the fifteenth chapter of John. "Everything that I learned from my Father I have made known to you." If self-disclosure is the secret to intimate and satisfying friendship, Jesus certainly took that step. I have always wondered whether the disciples responded in kind. Were they able to get past their disciple roles long enough to be friends with Jesus? Or were they hung up thinking of themselves as His servants even after He urged them into the transition to friendship?

Lord Jesus, I thank you for your offer of friendship. Please teach me what that means in my relationship with you. Help me not to be so occupied with obeying and serving you that I fail to learn how to enjoy you. Amen.

———————————

Take a moment to praise God and list those special friends in your life:

———————————

The Master Baker

BERYL HENNE

For it is God who works in you to will and to act according to his good purpose.
Philippians 2:13, *NIV*

I love to bake. Making a cake is one of the ways I can relax and show love to others at the same time.

I watched the other day as I stirred the batter. First came the sugar and butter. As they were beaten together, they took on a different shape, color and consistency. Then came the egg. What a mess it seemed at first!

Soon it was time to add the flour. It looked so white and clean, but was swallowed up almost immediately. I added raisins and nuts. Everything was losing its identity. The butter was no longer yellow, the flour white, nor the raisins brown—everything was a sickly beige.

It reminded me of a time in 1984 when God asked me to change my life-style. I protested, "No, Lord, I'll lose my identity! I'll lose all my color, my reputation, my fun! I'll be a nobody."

But God put changes in my life anyway—and I continued to cry out against them. He asked me to do things I didn't want to do. I was unwilling to be swallowed up, uncomfortable, unrecognizable for the Lord's sake.

Thankfully, He has continued to work in my life. In much the same way as I took the butter and the flour and made a cake out of it, so God has taken my life and is making something good out of it. He slowed me down so I would learn to know Him. He has given me a message, a song, a purpose—none of which I had before.

A cake is mixed and baked, then eaten and gone. But with God, He's still busy changing and making improvements. He's not finished with me yet!

Dear Father, I'm so glad that you are the Master Baker. Thank you for being in the business of making something good out of our lives—especially mine. Amen.

Let It Shine

ELOISE BUSHA

Ye are the light of the world.
Matthew 5:14, *KJV*

Have you ever gotten out of bed in the middle of the night and stumbled into the darkness, perhaps stubbing your toe against the bed or dresser? Many times, while my children were babies, I heard them cry out in the night and I jumped out of bed to run to their sides. More than once, I brandished a sore toe from my careless stumblings in the dark.

How much better it would have been for me to have kept a small flashlight by my bedside for unexpected midnight excursions. Nowadays, when the grandchildren spend the night, I leave a small nightlight on in their room.

It's amazing how much light a tiny bulb can give. Not only does this tiny light protect me from stubbing my toes in the darkness, but the children also benefit from its rays. They draw comfort from its presence as fears of darkness are dispelled.

Isn't that what our light of the world, Jesus, does for us when we accept Him as our personal Savior? He casts out darkness, dispels our fears, comforts us and shows us the way. And, once we accept Him and the light He has to offer, we too become little lights shining out in the dark world, giving love and comfort to others.

But we must not forget the source of our light. Just as an electric light switch must be connected to a power source in order to bring light into a room, so must we be connected to our source of energy in order to let our light shine. We must stay "plugged in" through constant communication to our Lord Jesus Christ, our Source.

Lord Jesus, I want to keep my power lines connected to you at all times, so that your light may shine through me. Amen.

Nobody Came

ELAINE WRIGHT COLVIN

Many guests were invited, and when the banquet was ready he sent messengers to notify everyone that it was time to come. But all refused! Matthew 22:3, *TLB*

I gave a party and no one came. It was unbelievable! Things like that only happen in bad dreams. Or, so I thought.

A quick glance around the room had revealed that all was in readiness. The party table was set: coffee pot, punch bowl, three dozen donuts, chips and dip, veggies. The chiming of the clock revealed that the doorbell should be ringing any minute to announce the arrival of my expected guests. But, as the minutes ticked away, it never rang.

Hours later, I was still pacing the floor, watching the clock and rearranging flowers. Disappointment numbed my senses. I stared at the empty living room, which should have been buzzing with the interaction of at least a dozen people. I wanted to scream, "Why? What went wrong?"

In the lingering hours of disappointment and quiet, God spoke softly to my heart. "Many people have done the same thing to me."

What? How could this be?

"Remember the Scripture that tells you about my banquet table, heavily laden, bidding you to come, eat, drink, and partake of the abundant life I am offering?"

"Yes, Lord. How many times have I ignored your invitation to come?"

It was sobering to realize that God surely feels the same regret, despair and dismay that I did.

My simple party was intended to reach out—a chance to share and fellowship around common interests. But no one came. Why? What excuses would I hear? Time pressures, scheduling problems, families, other priorities and obligations, health, inclement weather—all would doubtless be among the reasons.

Do my answers sound as feeble to God when I crowd Him out of my busy life? He offers so much: peace, joy, love, contentment. Yet, I often neglect His invitation.

The doorbell jarred me away from my thoughts. "Sorry I missed the party. I'm on my way home from PTA and I need to talk to someone for a minute. Am I too late?"

Father, forgive us for our preoccupation with the many activities that crowd our day. Help us to set right priorities and to remember it's never too late to accept your offers of peace, joy and the abundant life. Amen.

... Total Reliance

Hey, Remember Me?

LINDA MONTOYA

*I will not forget you! See, I have engraved you
on the palms of my hands.*
Isaiah 49:15,16 *NIV*

Rushing into the post office during the Christmas season, I saw John. He was the man who had often stopped me in the church parking lot or waited after my Bible study classes to chat.

"Hi, John," I said with enthusiasm.

He turned and looked at me, then hesitated. "Do I know you?"

"It's me, Linda! You know, from church!"

His eyes grew large. "Is it really you? You certainly have changed! I didn't recognize you."

Suddenly, I realized it was my weight gain. Only three months before, I had started a new job and was injured the first week at work. The pains in my back

81

and leg were excruciating. I had great fears of being hurt again, so I limited my physical activity. Work hours were extended. Job stress was tremendous. No breaks, sometimes no lunch. I neglected my nutritional needs. Chocolate became my escape. In only three months, I had gained enough weight to become unrecognizable to John.

As I left the post office in tears, I began to see a parallel in my spiritual life. How often had I withdrawn when injured? Filled with pain and full of fear of being hurt again, I had put up a wall. I had fed myself on negative thoughts, rehearsing past resentments, searching for ways of escape.

With my back and leg injury, I finally sought the help of a physical therapist, someone to walk with me through the pain, to challenge me to become strong again through exercise and proper eating habits.

In my spiritual life, I have learned to seek a Comforter, a Helper—the Holy Spirit, perhaps also a Christian friend—someone to invite me out of my pain and challenge me to continue to grow.

Thank you, Lord, for remembering me even when I make wrong choices. Amen.

. . . Our Fruitfulness

Nothing but Leaves

PEG RANKIN

Wherefore by their fruits ye shall know them.
Matthew 7:20, *KJV*

Our home in Michigan boasted 32 pear trees, which years earlier were part of a very productive orchard. When homes were built on the original farmland, the trees kept producing the same way they always had—abundantly. And I, having been endowed with a strong concept of stewardship, felt an accountability for every pear produced on my property. But the task became overwhelming.

One day, when I could no longer in good conscience offer any more pears to my friends or personally squeeze another pear into a jar or into the kids' lunchboxes, I cried in desperation, "Stop producing, trees! Stop producing!" But the command went totally unheeded. The trees did not stop making pears. They couldn't. They were fruit trees and fruit trees are programmed to produce fruit.

So it is with Christians—or is supposed to be. We who are connected to the Vine are expected to produce fruit of the Spirit—love, joy, peace, longsuffering, gentleness, goodness, faithfulness, meekness and self-control (see Gal. 5:22,23)—no matter what our circumstances happen to be.

Unfortunately, most of us put our efforts into leaves. We become more interested in participating in activities than we do in developing character. We sing in the choir, serve on boards and make brownies for the women's society. But our tempers get short and our nerves frazzled. Where is love for that difficult co-worker? Or joy in the midst of stress? Or peace that passes understanding? Or longsuffering toward the one who is causing us pain? Or control of our tempers and our tongues?

When Jesus was on His way from Bethany to Jerusalem, He caught sight of a fig tree that produced nothing but leaves (see Mark 11:13). Knowing His Father's law that "Every tree that bringeth not forth good fruit is hewn down and cast into the fire" (Matt. 7:19, *KJV*), Jesus cursed the non-producing tree.

If Jesus were to approach us today looking for fruit, I wonder how we would fare.

Oh, God, help me to get past my Christian activities and into a deeper relationship with you. I want to produce your likeness. In Jesus' name, Amen.

Pass the Oxygen, Please

MARTHA BOLTON

But they that wait upon the Lord shall renew their strength; they shall mount up with wings as eagles; they shall run, and not be weary; and they shall walk, and not faint.
Isaiah 40:31, *KJV*

I'm not what you'd call an exercise fanatic. Oh, I manage to do a few stretches every now and then. (It's the only way I can reach all the good items at a salad bar!) And I can do push-ups. But I don't think they count if you're doing them into your pillow!

See, I'm the type of person who wears pearls with sweats, and asks clerks if Reeboks come in a pump.

There was a time, though, when I paid more attention to my physical fitness. I was—how should I put it—very nearly in shape. Back then, I could buy an exercise video and keep up with it beyond pushing the *play* button. And when I jogged, cars would honk at me to sort of cheer me on. These days, the only time a car honks at me is when my collapsed body is blocking the intersection!

But that's the price I've paid for neglecting a regular exercise program. It takes me three light changes to make it across the street, and my strength just isn't what it used to be. In fact, the other day, I tried one of those machines where you put in a quarter and squeeze the handle to test your grip. Now, I'm not saying I registered *wimpy*, but I think I had a tighter grip on the quarter!

And, you know, my spiritual muscles need a regular exercise program, too, so they don't lose their strength. If I neglect them through a lackadaisical prayer life and a when-I-get-around-to-it attitude of Bible study, what kind of spiritual strength will I have when I need to call upon it? Will I be able to run and not be weary? Will I be able to walk and not faint?

Or will I just collapse under the stress?

Lord, help me not to neglect my spiritual fitness, that I may always stand strong in you. Amen.

. . . Trust and Obedience

Not the Whys, but the Way

MARIAN WIGGINS

What is that to you? You must follow me.
John 21:22, *NIV*

It was over a decade ago, in another state and, it seems now, another lifetime. I was a consultant in a large consulting firm. The other consultants and I enjoyed our jobs and each other. Our boss set the tone for the office—lively discussions filled with delightful humor. There was a sense of oneness as we weekly planned ways to help our clients creatively solve problems and experience success.

Then the unthinkable happened. Our boss—a loving, caring man—was called to fill a position in another city. The man who came to replace him seemed the very antithesis of our beloved former leader. The closest our new boss ever came to a smile was a mild scowl. He viewed any closeness between employees with an eye of suspicion, and seemed to count our clients as enemies who schemed to trip us up at every turn. Our weekly planning sessions quickly deteriorated to a series of barked commands. The tension in the office was so thick that some days it seemed you could reach out and feel its sharp, rough edges.

As I set out each day to the various cities in my territory, I often blinked back tears of humiliation and resentment. "Lord, why is this man here? Your Word says that there is no authority except that which you have established. Why, Lord, why have you put this man over us?" The silence in the car was deafening.

For several months my hurt and resentment built up until I was beginning to feel anger toward this new boss. And so were my fellow workers. But most of all, we were afraid of his outbursts of temper. When we were in the office, we seldom poked our heads out of our individual offices. If we had to consult a colleague, we found ourselves tiptoeing down the corridor to each other.

And then one evening I read a passage in my Bible I had read many times before. Up to that point, that particular portion of Scripture had never ministered to a personal need of mine. But it did that night—and has on many occasions since then.

The passage is in John. Jesus is talking to Peter and indicates the kind of death Peter will experience. Peter looks over at John and asks, "Lord, what about him?" Jesus replies, "If I want him to remain alive until I return, what is that to you? You must follow me."

Suddenly, my repeated question of, "Why, Lord,

why have you put this man over us?" was answered. "What is that to you? You must follow me." It boils down to the words *trust* and *obey*. I must trust His appointments and seek not the whys but the way of the path on which I am to follow Him.

Lord God, you are perfect love, and so I can trust that what you are doing is for the ultimate good. I commit my life anew to following you in trust and obedience. Amen.

———————

Take a moment to praise God and list things you've accepted by faith:

Pruning Hurts, Lord, but Don't Stop!

BERIT KJOS

I am the true vine, and my Father is the gardener. He cuts off every branch in me that bears no fruit, while every branch that does bear fruit he prunes so that it will be even more fruitful. John 15:1,2, *NIV*

Last year seethed with commitments and responsibilities. The phone rang incessantly. Now I work at home, alone—and wish they still needed me to teach, organize, counsel—anything.

Why did I resign? Did I misunderstand God's guidance?

Last year I missed the precious days alone with my King. I longed for quiet. Now I am free to study, write, meditate and delight in my best Friend. Then why this restlessness? O God, heal this ache inside me! I feel worthless, useless, a failure. What did I do wrong?

A memory flashed across my mind, interrupting my thoughts. I recalled a splendid grapevine stretching in the Israeli sunshine. Its long branches, heavy with ripening fruit, rested on rocks, inches above the ground.

I'm a branch of another Vine, and my purpose is to produce fruit for Him. I, His branch, am inseparably imbedded in the Vine, and the sap (the life-giving blood of the Vine) flows through my every cell, cleansing, nourishing and building.

Harvest comes—and goes. My fruit was taken, my leaves died. Suddenly my branch appears empty, dry and lifeless. Worse yet, the Vinedresser prunes away my long shoots—those that looked most promising and produced the sweetest grapes. Ouch! That hurt! Only a stump remains. I feel ugly and useless. Just yesterday I looked beautiful, productive and competent. Now I am reduced to total inadequacy. What happened?

The Vinedresser knows. If left, those long, strong shoots would produce lovely leaves in abundance, but little or no fruit to the glory of the Vine. The deeper He cuts, the more I depend on the Vine alone. Stripped bare, I turn my heart fully back to Him, my Source of Life.

The Vine felt the pain of the pruning with me; for what cut me, cut Him, as well. Together, we hurt, weep, heal and grow. Gently, He points me toward our common purpose and gives me hope and a vision. We must prepare to produce nourishing fruit—not beautiful foliage.

Again I rest in the all-sufficient Vine, confident

that His life flowing through me will produce a new crop. I simply believe what He shows me about Himself—and surrender to Him. His life in and through me never fails!

Teach me to trust your plan, precious Lord, while you prune, trim and direct. Make rest and surrender my habitual life-style. Amen.

My Kite

DIANTHA AIN

My faith is a kite
    That soars so high,
It cannot be seen
    By the naked eye.

It carries me with it
    Above the veil,
Sloughing my pain
    With its dancing tail,

Searching for paths
    Where the Saints have trod,
Yearning to land
    In the hand of God.

. . . Our Time and Organization

One-Woman Juggler

NICOLE HILL

Not by might, nor by power, but by my spirit, saith the Lord of hosts. Zechariah 4:6, *KJV*

Like most women today, I lead an active life. Often, I feel like a one-woman juggling act. Sometimes, it gets out of control—or, rather, I get out of control.

Recently, I found myself waking up in the morning, dreading to face the new day and my seemingly endless chores and duties. My prayer time was suffering because I felt so overwhelmed with pressures and responsibilities. Yet, I kept taking on more and more.

Then, one morning, I glanced down at a note pad a friend had given me for Christmas. It said, *One day at a time.* Seeking God's guidance, I sat down and made a list of the things I truly needed to accomplish that day. I didn't worry about what I had failed to do yesterday, or what I hoped to do tomorrow. I just concentrated on today.

As the day progressed (beginning with a renewed and refreshed prayer time), I found time to straighten my home, attend a friend's funeral, visit with a neighbor, do my marketing, work in the garden, and even spend a little time on my writing. As I climbed into bed that night, I looked at my list and smiled. I was right on schedule.

Lord, help me to remember it's not by my power, nor by my might, but by your Spirit that we accomplish anything worthwhile. Amen.

Take a moment to praise God and list ways to organize your day:

Putting Away Childish Things

EUGENIA PRICE

When I was a child, I talked like a child, I
thought like a child, I reasoned like a child.
1 Corinthians 13:11, *NIV*

Do you still talk like a little girl? That is, do you speak before you think? Do you know what you're talking about before you say the words, or do you just chatter thoughtlessly and aimlessly the way a little girl does?

Do you speak from knowledge or from ignorance? Do you speak from God-given insight about both divine and human nature? Or do you prattle without waiting quietly before God for His sure word concerning the situation, the Scripture or the person involved? Do you speak from inner fear and doubt as a little girl has a right to do? Or do you speak from inner confidence, built into your heart as a result of time spent with the God who has promised to care for you? Do you speak caustically or carelessly—the words springing haphazardly from the extremist side of your nature? Are you rigid and unyielding because like a little girl, you have just taken someone else's word for a matter and haven't bothered to think it through yourself? Are you thoughtless, even cruel, because you have been so busy with your own little doings you have forgotten how to think before you speak? Are you quick to cut someone down to size because that person somehow seems to have bested you in a real or imagined competition?

Little girls do all these things and it is normal for them to do them.

You and I are women. We are no longer little girls—in years, at least. It is not only immature and unchristian, it is downright ridiculous for harsh, thoughtless, cutting words to come from the mouth of a woman on whose face are the marks of her years! Years that should have proven to her (if her mirror hasn't) that it is time to *grow up.*

If we have truly put away childish things, if we are really through with them, we face facts as they are. Children face facts as they wish they were, not as they are. This kind of mature viewpoint will increase the capacity for peace in any woman—young or old, professional woman or housewife. It will move us steadily and creatively through the routine days and through the crisis times. *We discover how to lay hold of peace as we discover the freedom of maturity.*

Father, help us to let go of childish things and to seek maturity in your love. Amen.

The Bottom Line

BERYL HENNE

I will instruct you and teach you in the way you should go; I will counsel you and watch over you. Psalm 32:8, *NIV*

It was raining and windy in San Francisco. My husband was attending a seminar and I had the day to myself. Sitting before the fireplace in my hotel room, I was eager to enjoy a cozy fire while I did some writing. There were two big logs on the grate, the fireplace was equipped with gas jets to start the blaze; but, in spite of an hour of effort, it would not start for me!

In quiet desperation, I checked everything over carefully one more time. The damper was open, the logs were propped for maximum air flow, the jets were burning well, but the logs would not catch fire. Then I noticed something. On the wall beside the fireplace was a little white card. The last line read: *See that the vents in the bottom of the fireplace door are left open to allow the fire to get adequate draft.*

So that was it! I opened the vents and soon I was enjoying the anticipated cozy atmosphere of a room with a fire burning in the fireplace. As I sat, gazing into the dancing red and orange flames, I thought of how I was operating in my daily life. The big things seemed to be taken care of. I went to church and Sunday School. I served on committees. I prayed. But I was neglecting the instructions God had provided for me—I had not yet read the bottom line.

Just as I could not enjoy the fire until I had followed the printed instructions, so I cannot enjoy God until I read His Word and take time to follow His instructions. Until I realized those vents existed, I could not open them. In the same way, until I realize what God is asking me to do, I cannot obey Him.

Dear Father, please forgive me for all the times when I don't allow you to give me your instructions. I want to be teachable. Amen.

. . . Clean Hearts

I Don't Do Windows

KATHI MILLS

There is nothing concealed that will not be disclosed, or hidden that will not be made known. Luke 12:2, NIV

I hate housework. And I don't do windows—or wash baseboards, or clean closets, or polish silver, or check behind the furniture for cobwebs. Not very often, anyway. Oh, once or twice a year when out-of-town relatives are coming for a visit I do all that stuff—but I still hate it.

If I ever write a best-seller, the first thing I'll do is hire a housecleaner. Not a housekeeper—a housecleaner. You see, I keep my house very neat all the time—I just don't *clean* it.

What this means is that a burglar will never break into my house some morning after I've gone to work and find unmade beds, unwashed dishes, newspapers scattered across the floor, or unfolded towels in the bathroom. He will not become disgusted at the sight of toothpaste or whiskers in the sink. Nor will he feel nauseous from looking at three-day-old food encrusted on the burners of my stove.

But pity the poor guy if he has any allergies and decides to go rummaging around in the back of one of my dusty closets. And if he tries to escape through a window, I hope he's wearing gloves. The last time I went near my windows with Windex and a squeegee, I got sick and changed my mind. Much easier to just keep the curtains closed.

Which brings me to my point. Could it be that I live my spiritual life the way I clean house? Do I just do "surface cleaning" so I will appear holy and spiritual to others? Am I ignoring all those dirty corners—all those filthy cupboards and closets?

Because if I am, it won't do any good. When Jesus comes for me, He won't call ahead to let me know He's coming. There won't be any time for cleaning then. Everything I've tried to keep hidden will be brought to light. And I'll be so embarrassed.

Guess I'd better change my ways—and start doing windows.

Search the hidden corners of my heart, Lord, and make me willing to be truly cleansed by your forgiveness. Amen.

Published first in December 1986 by *Joyful Woman* magazine.

Rehearsing for the Real Thing

CAROL BECKERDITE

Wives, submit to your husbands as to the
Lord. For the husband is the head of the wife
as Christ is the head of the church, his body,
of which he is the Savior.
Ephesians 5:22,23, *NIV*

At 37, after eight years of being a widow and a single parent to my two children, I was getting married again. As I moved nervously through the wedding rehearsal, my mind already darting ahead to the *real thing*, I realized suddenly that marriage itself is only a rehearsal for the real wedding—our wedding in heaven to our true Bridegroom, the Lord Jesus Christ.

What other relationship on earth has as much potential to develop character? Where else can you find so many opportunities for wills to clash and tempers to flare? The Lord has called us to be submissive

101

to one another, at times yielding our rights. Marriage is indeed the supreme testing ground.

Most of our anger comes from what we perceive to be an infringement of our rights. But marriage demands that we take *I* and *me* off the throne, and become *we*. Every decision that is made affects our mutual union. There is no room for rigidity or large egos.

There are few things more inspiring than seeing a couple who knows their rights and responsibilities in the Lord and flows together in them. The power of agreement between husband and wife is awesome!

Each time we yield to the other person, we are being refined and perfected. Bondage exists when our natures are in conflict with God's nature. No wonder we are unhappy when we selfishly seek to get our own way and desires!

I shook my head and came out of my reverie. The rehearsal was almost over. Very soon it would be time for the real thing. I thanked God for my marriage to my earthly bridegroom—and for the heavenly marriage yet to come.

Father, give us a heart that lovingly yields to others that we might become a pure and spotless bride for our true Bridegroom. Amen.

Take
A
MOMENT
A
DAY
to learn about God . . .

. . . Through Family Members
We Learn About . . .

... How We Use Our Time

Baby Demands

KATHY COLLARD MILLER

There is an appointed time for everything. And there is a time for every event under heaven. Ecclesiastes 3:1, *NASB*

When my daughter, Sandy, was a few months old, she demanded constant attention. I didn't even get a break during her naps because she napped while she nursed. Discouraged, I looked around at my increasingly messy house and had nightmarish visions of this little dictator daughter controlling my life forever.

I felt depressed and hopeless. *She's always going to demand my attention every second!* I thought. *I'm never going to be loosed from these demands! Oh, Lord, why did I ever want to be a mother?*

And then a friend suggested I wake up in the morning planning to hold Sandy all day if need be. Then, if she didn't need me, I should regard it as a bonus, rather than a right entitled to me.

The next day I decided to hold Sandy as much as necessary and read a book to pass the time. Well, wouldn't you know it? Sandy took a long nap in her crib! I was disappointed. I didn't have an excuse to read my book.

I learned that day that children sense when we are anxious to be free of their demands. If we will meet their needs, they will sense security, which will make them less demanding.

On the other hand, children shouldn't rule our lives. There needs to be a balance. There will be times when baby must wait. It is up to us to make wise choices based on our baby's development. This may mean fixing a simpler meal later than expected, when the baby is sleeping or less fussy.

I found a baby carrier very helpful during those times. Sandy felt close to me and received the security she needed.

Little by little, I used the baby carrier less often. Sandy stopped needing me constantly and could play by herself in her crib. Then she could crawl and explore. Eventually she walked and then played with friends.

Now Sandy is 13 and I have more freedom. She is very independent and loves to be with her friends. When I think of those times when she demanded so much of me, I remember a time of closeness. With the perspective of passing time, what seemed like a dismally long period was actually quite short. The attention I grudgingly gave now becomes love I'm glad I shared.

Father, help me to give as much love as I can when you give me the opportunity. Amen.

Correction Without Rejection

BARBARA COOK

For the Lord will not reject his people.
Psalm 94:14, *NIV*

P atti was telling me about her job in a group home for troubled girls. Around Christmas time, Patti was assigned the duty of calling each girl's family to make arrangements for the girl to visit during the family's celebrations. To her dismay, several mothers refused to allow their daughters to come home at all. Others replied with something like, "She can come for Christmas Day, but no longer!"

Patti felt sickened and sad as she realized, for the first time in her life, that it was actually possible for parents to deeply reject their own children. And she began to appreciate her parents more. "No matter what, I knew my mom and dad would always love me," she said.

This made me think about my own parents and the unconditional love and acceptance they have always given. But I keep meeting women who didn't have parents like Patti's or mine. These women had the kind of parents who traded love for good performance. And they traded rejection for failure. In fact, in many homes, even Christian homes, rejection is a favorite means of discipline.

This encourages me to think about my own parenting. Do I have ways of disciplining my children that come across as rejection? Those of us who hold high expectations for our kids because we believe in biblical standards of right and wrong can have a tough time when a child does something that violates our standards or embarrasses our theology.

Knowing that my heavenly Father will never reject me is such good news! If I do something stupid today, He won't shake His head at me and say, "That's it for you, kid! I've had it!" To know He will correct me brings security and confidence. I can dare to think, to try new adventures and risk caring about people. If I happen to steer in an errant direction, my Father will warn me and help me correct my course. But it's easier for me to receive correction in any situation, whether it's a driver's training course or a piano lesson, when I know that correction won't be dished out in insulting, demeaning words. If I am safe with the Teacher, I can receive warnings and suggestions without defensiveness. When my Heavenly Parent says, "Here's a better way—try this, Barb!" I can respond, not with shame or despondency, but happily, glad to know He's teaching me.

Dear Father, I thank you for correcting and teaching me in such kind, non-rejecting ways. Help me to follow your example when I correct and teach my children. Amen.

My Shepherd
DIANTHA AIN

The Lord is my shepherd;
He shows me the way.
I follow Him faithfully
Day after day.
His guiding power
Is strong and clear,
As if He were whispering
Into my ear.
He's patient and kind
When I stumble or fall.
He loves me completely,
My flaws and all.
If I lose my focus
Now and then,
He lures me back
To His path again.
The Lord is my shepherd
Through storm and through strife,
And my shepherd He'll be
For the rest of my life.

. . . God's Faithfulness

Don't Forget!

DAISY HEPBURN

Yes, I will bless the Lord and not forget the glorious things He does for me.
Psalm 103:2, *TLB*

Grandpa Eric—my father—sat unmoved and unresponsive as we entered his plain but comfortable room at the nursing home. Familiar faces smiled from the photos stuck into the framed mirror of the small dresser.

"Here we are, Grandpa, every one of us!" they seemed to call out. We had tucked them close by as reminders of the love that surrounded our saintly—but sinking—grandfather.

"We're glad to see you again." "How are you feeling?" "Isn't it a lovely day?" The greetings and enthusiasm were one-sided, and we continued to keep up the cheerful banter of conversation with family news. The time went quickly, and soon we were gathering up sweaters and purses, getting ready to leave once again.

"Will you pray with us, Grandpa, before we leave?"

"Heavenly Father . . . " His voice quivered with the effects of Alzheimers, but the conviction of his shining faith broke through the darkness of his mind. He remembered without a pause the names of his dear wife, each child and grandchild—and he prayed.

My father has gone on to heaven now, but when I remember him, I reflect on our gracious God who allowed a certain saint the privilege of remembering that which really mattered.

How comforting to know that the Holy Spirit helps us remember all the forget-me-nots planted in the garden of our hearts!

Lord, today help me to remember that you will not forget me. Amen.

Take a moment to praise God and list fond memories:

Laundry and Apple Pie

CHRISTINE RICH

And God is able to make all grace abound to you, so that in all things at all times, having all that you need, you will abound in every good work. 2 Corinthians 9:8, *NIV*

U gh, what a morning," I groaned, trudging over to the kitchen counter. I had tossed and turned all night, finally falling asleep just before the alarm blared in my ear.

I reached over the counter and wearily flipped over a page of my daily devotional calendar. I read about the gifts God had given me and how I should share them with others.

I flung open a cabinet door. "What gifts could I possibly have to give to anyone today?" I muttered, while scanning the shelves. "And what in the world am I going to make for dessert?"

I spotted the shortening. Apple pie flashed through my mind. I pulled the can toward me. Lowering it to the counter, memories flowed through me. I remembered how my friend Martha had made pies as her gift to her family. A smile tugged at the corners of my mouth. "Hmm, this pie could be my gift for dinner tonight."

I assembled it and slid the finished product into the hot oven. Heading down into the basement to check on the laundry, I noticed a slight spring in my step. As I began putting the wet clothes into the basket, Daisy, our multi-breed mutt, trotted up and nudged my hand. I reached over and scratched her ears. Her laughing mouth and dancing eyes increased my feeling of well-being.

Dropping the final article of clothing into the basket, I lifted the load and walked briskly out to the clothesline with Daisy prancing along beside me. As I clipped the first garment to the line, I thought of my grandmother. She had taught me how to hang clothes. That had been her gift to me.

I fastened the last piece of wash to the line, then ran into the house and turned off the oven buzzer. Slowly, I removed the hot, steaming pie from the oven. The odor of cooked apples and cinnamon permeated the air. I sniffed the sweet aroma and glanced out the window to see the clothes flapping lazily in the breeze.

"What a beautiful day, God! Thank you for sending me the warm memories of my grandmother and Martha—and for helping me to see that I do have gifts to share, after all."

Heavenly Father, when I feel down, help me to remember the gifts of others, and to remember also that by giving, I uplift my own spirit. Amen.

A Passion for Giving

MARY BECKWITH

Let each one do just as he has purposed in his heart; not grudgingly or under compulsion; for God loves a cheerful giver.
2 Corinthians 9:7, *NASB*

I've never seen anyone quite like her. Her greatest enjoyment in life is to give to others. I don't dare compliment her on something she has or she'll give it to me! I've heard others say, "Oh, Catherine, I really like that dish!" And she'll say, "It's yours!" She'll give away practically anything to nearly anyone.

My sister and I tease my mother. We say, "Well, from now on, we'll just buy you Christmas and birthday gifts that we like 'cause we usually get everything back anyway!"

Apparently she's always been that way. I can remember as a little girl hearing people say, "Catherine would give you the shirt off her back."

And I used to be scared she really would! My literal child-mind would picture her running around in her underwear.

She delights in shopping—for everyone but herself. But all her gifts are not purchased. She does all kinds of handiwork and gives most of that away, too. Attached to many of these items is a little tag which says, "Specially Made by Catherine."

Whenever I go to visit her, I always come home with more than I started out with. It wasn't so bad when I lived in Michigan and had my car to transport things—I'd always end up with a trunkful! But now I live in California and fly to see her. On my last visit, my suitcase bulged with nylon stockings, a new blow dryer, foods I can't get out West, socks for my husband, shirts for the boys and Tupperware for my daughter. I even brought a Crockpot back in my carry-on luggage!

Every once in a while, the UPS man delivers a *care* package from her—usually full of suprises, such as kitchen items, perfume, Combos snacks, Betty Crocker Date Bars, and lots of hand-made items by none other than this dear lady herself—my mother.

A holiday doesn't go by without receiving a card in the mail from her. It almost always has something stuffed inside! For Mother's Day, I actually got a card from her, for heaven's sake!

What a heart! She gives her time, her talents, her entire being to make others happy—and just for the sheer joy of giving.

How privileged I am to be her daughter! Of course, I enjoy all the things she generously gives. But what I really want from her is just a portion of her passion for giving.

Heavenly Father, I thank you so much for my mother. She will probably never know how much I love and admire her. But what's most important is your love for her, for God loves a cheerful giver. Amen.

Take a moment to praise God and list blessings you've received from giving:

Why Does He Have to Suffer?

DIANE JUSTUS

*Praise be to the God and Father of our Lord
Jesus Christ, the Father of compassion and
the God of all comfort, who comforts us in all
our troubles, so that we can comfort those in
any trouble with the comfort we ourselves have
received from God. For just as the sufferings of
Christ flow over into our lives, so also through
Christ our comfort overflows.*
2 Corinthians 1:3-5, *NIV*

My dad was dying of cancer. Tightening
cycles of agony and hallucinations signaled his
impending death. Time was judged by the hours
between morphine shots; even then, these did not
lessen his pain.

"Why, God?" My tears flowed continuously as I
grasped for hope in the midst of despair. "Why does
he have to suffer?"

Rubbing his thin hands and caressing his fevered

brow, I sang to my dad and prayed for his peace. He was unconscious now, no longer aware of my presence or even of his pain. Trying to find meaning in the midst of it all, I thought back on his illness and realized that he had suffered only to a point—admittedly far past where I would have chosen—then he either lost consciousness or improved temporarily. God's grace was sufficient for him in his suffering.

We, as his family, had suffered with him during those long years, but sitting there next to him in that hospital room, I realized the changes that had taken place within us. We were less fearful, more hopeful, and our faith had been strengthened. We had faced suffering and death, yet because of God's grace, we were not defeated. The fiery hand of suffering had done its work in helping us mature.

When my dad was asked, "Why should *you* have to suffer?" his answer was, "Why not me?" I began to think, *Yes, why not us?* God has promised to go through our trials and sufferings with us, revealing Himself more clearly. He said that if we will stay lovingly pliable and not become bitterly brittle, we will reap rich rewards. So, why not us? Why do we count the comfort of our ease more important than the comfort that flows from Christ? Why not us? We will know Him far better when we allow Him to draw us into the fellowship of His suffering, whether the suffering be for others or within ourselves. Either way, it is a glorious fellowship.

Lord, help us to know you in the fellowship of your suffering, for our goal is to be like you. May we know your peace and joy in the midst of our trials. Amen.

Uninvited Guests

MARLENE ASKLAND

All things work together for good to them that love God. Romans 8:28, *KJV*

Having been a pastor's wife for many years, I'm used to uninvited guests. In fact, under most conditions, I'm delighted to have them.

However, when our uninvited guests turned out to be cockroaches, I was appalled! And had I known when I first saw the creepy, crawly little critters that they would be around for an entire year, I probably would have packed up and moved out myself!

Cockroaches—the very word sounded dirty. I just wanted to be rid of them before anyone found out! But spraying pesticides in our home was impossible because it could have had disastrous results for one of my daughters. So we went about trying to extermi-

119

nate them by trapping them in cockroach traps—a safe but slow process.

One day during that year as I was praying about the situation, a Scripture popped into my head: *All things work together for good.* I almost laughed out loud. Cockroaches? Well, Lord, if you say so . . . .

Several weeks after the disappearance of the last cockroach, our daughter, who had just left home as a missionary to Paraguay, wrote to us:

> "Mom, do you remember all those awful cockroaches we had? [How could I ever forget!] Well, we have huge, flying ones here! I'm glad I was able to get used to them at home before coming to Paraguay."

God had used even my uninvited guests for good. He had used them to help prepare my daughter for the mission field.

Thank you, Lord, for taking even the most adverse circumstances and using them for good. Amen.

... Healing and Restoration

Turning over the Reins

CAROL BECKERDITE

The fear of the Lord is the beginning of knowledge; fools despise wisdom and instruction. Proverbs 1:7, *NASB*

Eight years ago, when I first received Jesus into my heart, my husband was ill with cancer. He died a few weeks later. I became angry with God, blaming Him for my loss. If He was the God who could heal all, why hadn't He healed my husband?

I didn't realize it at the time, but I wasn't allowing God to work in my life. I was bound up with bitterness and unforgiveness. I was running away from God, yet I wasn't free or happy apart from Him.

A year or so later when I began dating, I felt very guilty if I was not moral and chaste in my relationships. I found I couldn't sin and be happy. I realize now that it was the convicting power of the Holy Spirit, ever drawing me back to my Lord.

Healing took place gradually as I started attending church regularly and reaching out for fellowship, prayer and support. I had to forgive God for what I perceived He had caused, and I had to pardon my husband for leaving me with two children, ages one and three.

When I finally met my present husband, I hadn't dated in three years. It had been a time of healing and restoration, a time of learning that all things do work together for good to those who love and serve the Lord (see Rom. 8:28).

I now know a peace and joy that is real and constant, but I had to turn the reins over to God in order to find them.

Thank you, Lord, for daily showing me the wisdom and simplicity of your ways. I thank you that you are a living God who loves and cares for each of us as if we were your only child. Amen.

If Only I Had Time!

INGRID SHELTON

There is a time for everything, and a season for every activity under heaven.
Ecclesiastes 3:1, *NIV*

Mom, could you alter my jeans, please?" my teenage daughter asked, coming into the kitchen. "I need to wear them tonight."

"Would you type my pocket charts for me, dear?" my husband asked, finishing his breakfast. "And, while you're at it, maybe you could type my report?"

I nodded silently.

"And don't forget to meet me at the bank just before three this afternoon," he added, going out the door.

Just then, the phone rang. "Could you drive me to the lawyer?" a friend asked urgently. "I have an appointment at ten."

I agreed, resentment rising within me. Besides these requests, I also had to clean, wash clothes, cook dinner, and shop for groceries—all before three o'clock! Didn't anyone realize I was working, too? That I considered free-lance writing a job? If only I had time, I would write a lot of stories, articles, even books! How I envied other writers who told of months of uninterrupted writing time, or of going away to a secluded hideaway somewhere just to write!

Finally, about 1:30, I sat down to write. Picking up my Bible to calm myself, I read Ecclesiastes 3:1. I stopped to meditate. What would Jesus have done in my place? I knew Jesus came to do the will of His Father. He did not please Himself. Jesus was never rushed nor hurried. Yet, He accomplished everything He was meant to do in just three short years.

I knew then that my family had to come first. It was a blessing to have them, to be needed. It really didn't matter if I wrote today or tomorrow. With God's help, I could make the most of those days I was able to write. And, most likely, the time would come when my family would be gone from home and I would have many more days to write. Surely I could wait for that time—God's time.

Dear Jesus, thank you for your example. Help me to put my priorities in right perspective. Amen.

Absence Makes the Heart Grow Stronger

ELIZABETH LARSON

And I will give them an heart to know me, that I am the Lord. Jeremiah 24:7, *KJV*

I'm a navy brat. You know, one of those kids who can have middling-income parents, along with four brothers, but who can still travel half the world before the age of ten. Childhood was an adventure. My brothers and I (and my parents, too) never knew where we would end up next. Mom would get a letter and say, "Guess what! Your father received his orders." Or Dad would come home one night and say, "Well, guess where we're going!"

Mom would pack the suitcases and Dad would lead the way. If we didn't have to get shots, my brothers and I followed happily, ready to explore our new home. But often, even before we could get settled, Dad would tell us (over dinner, eaten off of paper plates arranged on a trunk because the movers had lost our china and the dining room table), "Well, the ship is leaving tomorrow . . . . "

The next morning, he would kiss our long, sad faces and tell us to be good for Mom. Then he would leave—forever, it seemed. And, during that forever-absence, we would forget what it was like to live with Dad. He became a warm, pleasant memory whose picture smiled at us from the frame above Mom's desk.

Then, he would come home. And, after hugs, kisses and a reunion celebration, the poutings and tears would begin. The boys had to get their hair cut ("You're lucky you're a girl!" they'd mutter). And I was told to do better in math, a subject that never seemed to confuse my brothers. In short, Dad had become a stranger during his absence, and we grumbled about his renewed authority over us. There were also emotional ties that had to be strengthened because we had lost touch with one another's hearts.

It can be the same in my relationship with my heavenly Father. I get too busy. I forget to pray. Those special ties of the heart weaken and I forget that He has authority over me. My absences from Him cause our hearts to become as strangers. But, like my dad, God is a forgiving Father, always ready to renew our love.

I pray my heart will never become a stranger to you, Lord. Amen.

When Spam by Candlelight Isn't Enough

MARTHA BOLTON

Nevertheless I have somewhat against thee,
because thou hast left thy first love.
Revelation 2:4, *KJV*

I remember when I first started dating my husband. There was such excitement, such joy! And not just on my mother's part because I had finally found a boyfriend she didn't have to rent. But on my part, as well.

Everything had to be perfect. I wouldn't dream of letting him see me in curlers, without make-up, and with cold cream on so thick I'd look like a cream pie with eyebrows. In other words, I wouldn't dream of letting him see me the way he's seen me for the past 17 years of marriage!

Ah, how easy it is to become complacent in a relationship, to take the other party for granted.

Now, don't get me wrong. Our romance isn't dead. It's just that, nowadays, the only way I can get my husband's heart to skip a beat is to show him my MasterCard and VISA statements. And, sure, I still enjoy running my fingers through his hair, but lately it's just been to work in the Grecian Formula.

I think it's time I got back to that first love relationship. So, tonight when my husband comes home from work, he's not going to find me wearing the same flannel pajamas and armadillo bedroom slippers I had on this morning. I'm going to put on a dress and some make-up, and prepare a special dinner that up until now he's only dreamed about. I'm going to cook something edible.

See, all it takes is a little effort and determination to turn complacency into ecstasy.

And, you know, if we're not careful, our relationship with God can become complacent, too. Like a marriage, it needs the proper attention and commitment to grow into something beautiful. And, like a marriage, we may sometimes need to stop and get back to our first love.

Lord, refresh my spirit, renew my joy, and bring me back into a first love relationship with you. Amen.

Faithful Over a Few

DONNA FLETCHER CROW

*Who then is a faithful and wise servant, whom
his lord hath made ruler over his household, to
give them meat in due season?*
Matthew 24:45, *KJV*

Dear Lord, this morning our pastor told
how he's growing through extended times alone with
you and how he's learning from extensive Bible
study.

Lord, I'd like to spend long times apart with you
like that, but you know I have four children in four
schools this year, and it's all I can do just to keep
from drowning in dishes and laundry.

"But, my child, look at the beautiful children you
are rearing for me; and you do have a few minutes
alone with me each morning. You are serving where I
put you."

O Lord, thank you for accepting my widow's mite!

We all get frustrated with the routineness and seeming unimportance of our jobs. Other people are scaling the heights professionally, financially, spiritually. We would like to be in charge of all the Master's property now. Sometimes it helps to realize we are where we are as servants of the Master, and we are assigned to this task because it is important in His scheme of things.

Help me to see even my smallest task as a part of your great scheme, Lord. Give me the assurance that when I do whatsoever my hand finds to do, you are guiding my hand. Amen.

Take a moment to praise God and list tasks He has assigned to you:

. . . Clear Communication

Speaking the Truth in Love

KATHY COLLARD MILLER

Speaking the truth in love, we are to grow up in all aspects into Him. Ephesians 4:15, *NASB*

The incident stands out vividly in my mind. After being married for two years, Larry and I shopped for a new dinette set. I didn't care particularly what we bought, but I did have a strong, emotional vision of our future children nestled around the table doing their homework together. It was a wonderful expectation of closeness and family unity: children laughing, sharing their day, asking how to divide 42 by 7.

Larry, on the other hand, knew he wanted a distressed-wood table. I didn't know what that meant, but I soon found out. It meant the wood of the table surface was slightly pitted and grooved. I told him that was fine, and proceeded to describe my idealistic image of our children someday surrounding the table.

Larry responded, "But they can't use this table to do their homework."

I could barely keep my mouth from dropping open. *So he doesn't want the children to ruin his precious table, huh?*

I didn't say another thing. We bought the distressed-wood table. I pouted for a long time. It seemed to point out to me my husband's insensitivity to my needs—and to the needs of our future family.

It wasn't until years later that I could think about the incident more clearly. Suddenly, I realized what Larry had really meant—not that the children couldn't work at the table because they would damage it, but because the pitted wood would hamper their writing. I began to see how the entire misunderstanding could have been alleviated by one simple question: "Honey, what do you mean?"

Communication is a skill that requires us to stop thinking we know what the other person means. We may think we do, but words can have different meanings to different people.

Through the years I've learned to ask questions like, "Honey, are you saying . . . ?" or "What do you mean?" As a result, there haven't been as many misunderstandings in our house.

But what *is* in our house is that same distressed-wood dinette set. Sitting there, doing their homework, are our two children. They don't mind the pitted wood at all.

Lord God, give me wisdom so that my words will be truthful and yet gracious. Amen.

. . . God's Encompassing Love

A Child's Cry

SHIRLEY DOBSON

*In my distress I called upon the Lord, and
cried unto my God: he heard my voice out of
his temple, and my cry came before him, even
into his ears. Psalm 18:6, KJV*

I was the daughter of a confirmed alcoholic. Only those who have lived through this nightmare will understand the full implication of this experience. I could never ask a friend to spend the night for fear my father would return in a drunken stupor and embarrass me. Night after night, he would stumble home in the early morning hours, belligerent and foul-mouthed. We would be awakened by his shouting and threats and would often hide to avoid his wrath. The rooms of our home had been patched with brown butcher paper and painted over to conceal where he had shoved his fists through the walls in fits of anger.

It was only through the wisdom and devotion of my mother that I survived the emotional pressures of those years. She is a strong woman, and she marshaled all of her resources to hold our little family together. Since Dad spent his entire paycheck at the bar each Friday night, Mother went to work to support the family. She found a job at a fish cannery which required her to work unpredictable hours. Many times she would be called at three or four in the morning after having been kept awake all night by her harassing, drunken husband. I marveled at her ability to hold a job and to do the marketing, cooking, housekeeping and laundry under those stressful circumstances.

Most importantly, Mom convinced my brother and me that she loved us. And because of that love, she constantly sought ways to get us through those difficult years. She had the wisdom to know that she needed help in raising two rambunctious kids, and she turned for assistance to a local evangelical church. Mom would not go with us (Sunday was her "catch up" day), but she knew that churches offered more than one kind of salvation, and her children needed all the help they could get.

It was in that little neighborhood church that I was introduced to Jesus Christ, and invited Him into my heart and life. He became my special friend, and I've never been the same since that moment.

As I look back on the painful experiences of my childhood, I am overwhelmed with gratitude to God for answering my early prayers. He heard the desperate cries of a ten-year-old girl who could offer Him nothing in return. I had no status, no special abilities, no money to contribute. My father was not a physician or a lawyer or a member of the city council. I was totally without dignity or social influence. Yet the Creator of the Universe entered my little room and communed with me about the difficulties I was experiencing. It was awesome to realize that He loved me just as I was, and my pain became His pain. What a magnificent God we serve!

Thank you, Lord, that you are always listening for our cry. Thank you, too, for wiping away the tears from our eyes. Amen.

From *Let's Make a Memory,* by Gloria Gaither and Shirley Dobson, Copyright 1983; used by permission of Word Books, publisher, Waco, Texas.

Take a moment to praise God and list times He has comforted you:

... How to Accept Change

Expanding Roles

BONNIE WHEELER

*She watches over the affairs of her household
and does not eat the bread of idleness.*
Proverbs 31:27, *NIV*

When we were first married, Dennis and I planned that I would stay home with the children (we wanted at least four) and Dennis would provide for us.

For the first 15 years of our marriage we lived out that traditional dream. I loved having a spotless home and well-cooked meals. I made our clothes, baked our bread and did needlework. We eventually parented six children.

In 1977 I started writing during the baby's nap. It took some real schedule scrambling to pull it off but I managed to not let my writing change the family lifestyle.

Eventually I wrote more, started teaching at conferences and presenting my workshops on time stewardship. Trips away from home were limited to once or twice a month.

This past year our medical bills got out of hand and I started working part time at the local school. With those five mornings I lost my cherished flexibility, gained a whole new perspective on juggling my time and found a new respect for my working sisters.

I am grateful that I had those precious early years home with the children. I am also grateful for the way the Lord has brought me through in cycles so I haven't tried (or had to try) doing it all at once.

Father, help us to be open to change and flexible in your work. Amen.

Adapted from *The Hurrier I Go . . . Finding Time for the People in Your Life* by Bonnie Wheeler. © Copyright 1985 by Bonnie G. Wheeler. Published by Regal Books, A Division of GL Publications, Ventura, CA. All rights reserved. Used by permission.

Take a moment to praise God and list blessings that have come through change:

Fear, Fire and Wings

JUNE CURTIS

I will hide beneath the shadow of your wings until this storm is past. Psalm 57:1, *TLB*

As a child, some of my most vivid memories are of the creepy, crawly creatures I imagined at night as the darkness encompassed me. Fear of the seemingly real dragons, snakes and bogymen cavorting in the shadows of my room often kept me from going to bed. Since I had several siblings, there was a hard and fast rule against sleeping with our parents. I felt so alone as I pulled the blankets over my head and tucked them tightly around myself, until impending suffocation forced me to stick my face out and gasp for air.

One night, my grandmother invited me to stay with her, promising that I would be able to sleep with her. Her plump arms felt like pillows as she snuggled my small frame next to hers. At last, I confided my unspoken nighttime fears. That's when she told me a story that changed my life forever.

It seems as though Mother Hen took her baby chicks out into a field one day to scratch for grain. Her brood of about a dozen chicks soon learned which were the edible grains, and chirped excitedly as they scattered in search of more delectable fare.

Suddenly, Mother Hen smelled the rancid odor of smoke. She knew from experience that the smell of smoke was always accompanied by fire. As the smoke thickened, she became alarmed, realizing to her utter dismay that she and her little family were completely surrounded by flames.

Clucking loudly, she called her precious offspring to her side, then raised her wings and brought them down over the chicks, embracing them as tightly as possible.

Soon, the inevitable happened. The flames swept over Mother Hen and her brood.

As soon as it was safe, Farmer Jones went out into the field to assess the damage. While walking through the still smoking acreage, he saw something lying on the ground in front of him. Kicking at the object with his foot, he turned over the charred remains of Mother Hen. To his absolute amazement, out from under her burned body emerged the baby chicks, alive and unharmed.

Grandmother pointed out to me that just as those baby chicks could have chosen to shun their mother's protective wings, we, too, can choose to ignore God's offer of protection and be consumed by the fires and fears of this life. Or we can elect to completely trust Him and abide in His love and protection day and night. The choice is ours as He beckons us to His side.

It was then I first realized that if God loved me enough to die for me, He also loves me enough to take care of all my fears. Since that night with Grandma, I have always remembered that Jesus is my best and closest friend, and that, as Mother Hen encircled her family with her wings, so He covers me with His.

O Lord, may I never crawl out from the protection of your wings! Amen.

Take a moment to praise God and list times you've realized His protection:

... His Intimate Love

My Mary

MARY BECKWITH

The sheep hear his voice; and he calls his own sheep by name. John 10:3, *NASB*

I can hear him now. It's as if it were yesterday. Dad would cuddle me in his arms and say, "My Mary," and I would feel so special and so loved.

Dad died 15 years ago at the age of 53 from the ravages of cancer. My handsome, meticulous father, who was always so particular about his looks; many, in fact, say he resembled Clark Gable.

I'll never forget seeing him lying in his hospital bed just before that cold and dismal day in November, a remnant of the man he once was. I would have given anything for him to be able to say, "My Mary." But he never would again. Only memories now.

One day, not too long ago, I was in prayer, seeking God's comfort at a time when the responsibilities of life seemed just too much for me to handle. All of a sudden, I heard my name—I heard, "My Mary." And I knew it was my heavenly Father reaching down to me with His infinite love and comfort. I've heard those words several times since. Perhaps I'm conjuring them up in my mind, just wanting to relive moments of the past. I don't know for sure.

But one thing I do know. God tells me in His Word that He calls His sheep by name. He says, "Before I was born the Lord called me; from my birth he has made mention of my name" (Isa. 49:1, *NIV*). He is that intimate with His children. It's as if He reaches down with His loving arms, cuddles us and calls us each one by name.

I'm confident that when I'm ushered into heaven, God will reach out His arms and welcome me with the words, "My Mary." And I can picture Dad, once again young and virile, waiting not too far behind, with his arms outstretched, his lips forming those treasured words.

Dear Heavenly Father, thank you that you love your sheep so intimately that you call each one of us by name. And thank you for the promise that we will be reunited with precious loved ones when we come to spend eternity with you. Amen.

Take

A

MOMENT

A

DAY

to learn about God . . .

. . . Through the Eyes
of a Child
We Learn About . . .

... The Simplicity of His love

No Fireworks for Jesus

MARGARET BROWNLEY

*And whatsoever ye do in word or deed, do all
in the name of the Lord Jesus.*
Colossians 3:17, *KJV*

In 1976, my husband and I took our three children across the country to the East Coast to take part in our nation's gala Bicentennial celebration. This extravaganza featured spectacular parades, tall ships and colorful carnivals. We saw fantastic fireworks displays and tasted a piece of the largest birthday cake ever baked. Not a penny was spared to make this one of the most dazzling events ever.

After returning home, we asked each child to describe the most memorable part of our trip. One son said it was the night that we'd caught fireflies in a jar. Our second son mentioned the cow that had wandered over to our campsite one morning and helped

145

herself to Oreo cookies. Our daughter said her most memorable moment was watching the electrical storms. Fireflies, cows and electrical storms—all novelties to children raised in Los Angeles, to be sure, but hardly the sort of thing my husband and I had in mind when we set out to show our children the wonders of our country.

In this world of "bigger is better" it's hard to remember that it's the little things that make up the rich tapestry of our land, just as it's the little things that give meaning to our lives. A telephone call from a loved one, a smile from across the room, a walk in the moonlight—these are all treasures that can be tucked away in our memory banks to be brought out as needed and enjoyed anew.

Yet, when we're called to do God's work, we think in terms of greatness. How many hours have I wasted looking for the perfect gift to send a shut-in, for instance, when taking that person for a drive in the country might have meant so much more? How many times have I made a speech, when a single word like "sorry" would have made a greater impact? How often have I become so overwhelmed with the number of homeless or starving people that I've thought, What good will my humble offering do?

Jesus lived a simple life and spoke of simple truths. He never worried about getting His message across in bigger and better ways. He never worried about numbers or Nielsen ratings. There were no fireworks to mark His speeches, no gala celebrations to trace His progress, and yet, He managed to change the course of the world.

Lord, help me not to become distracted by commer-

146

cialism. *Let me remember that in dying on the cross, you taught us that the greatest gift we can give is ourselves. Amen.*

Summer's Gone
KATHI MILLS

Feet stuck to the floor from Popsicle drips,
planning and packing for family trips;
so many dishes in the sink—
must they use a clean glass for every drink?
I just can't take much more of this noise!
Why can't they ever pick up their toys?
The slamming door, the ringing phone—
if only I could be alone!

Then suddenly it's time for school;
no more beach or swimming pool.
Off they go, down the street,
sounds of laughter and running feet.
A sigh of relief, but wait! What's this?
A tear in my eye as I blow them a kiss.
Oh, Lord, it seemed to go so fast!
These special times just never last!

Teach me, Father, to value each day,
to live, to love, to laugh, to play.

His Was the Holy Bible

MARY BECKWITH

The testimony of the Lord is sure, making wise the simple. Psalm 19:7, *NASB*

The little boy sat next to his grandmother, behind me in church. Looking forward to the day when I can teach my grandchildren about Jesus and have them come to church with me, I listened to the service with one ear, the other tuned in to the little boy and his grandmother.

He was asking her about what the pastor was doing. She, very quietly and patiently, was explaining everything to him. I noticed he had brought his very own Bible, so when the pastor read from Scripture, the little boy tried to follow along. When the pastor announced he was reading from the *NIV* Bible, the boy seemed puzzled.

"What is the *NIV* Bible?" he asked his grand-mother. When she explained there are many different versions of the Bible, he proudly announced, "Mine's the *Holy* Bible!"

I smiled, tears welling up in my eyes. How precious are the words of little children! So honest, so uninhibited, so wise.

But his response struck a chord. It made me consider just how complicated we can make something so basic as Christianity. We add a lot of do's and don'ts, conditions, interpretations, varying opinions, many of which merely add up to division and confusion in the Body.

Karl Barth, author of volumes on Christianity, was asked to summarize in one sentence what Christianity was all about. He answered, "Jesus loves me, this I know, for the Bible tells me so."

How foolish all of the addenda look when we remember how basic God's love and grace really are. All of the stuff we've added along the way just doesn't matter when we consider simply that Jesus came as a baby, He lived among us, He died for our sins, then He rose again, all in fulfillment of God's redeeming grace.

I probably wouldn't even recognize that little boy if I were to see him again, but I will never forget his words: "Mine is the Holy Bible!"

And so is mine. Hallelujah!

Thank you, Lord Jesus, for your grace. Let me never forget that all I ever have to know is your simple yet profound love for me. I'm sorry for the times I've tried to complicate the basics of Christianity. Amen.

Because I Want To!

RUTH M. BATHAUER

The tax-gatherer, standing some distance away, was even unwilling to lift up his eyes to heaven, but was beating his breast, saying, "God, be merciful to me, the sinner!"
Luke 18:13, NASB

My sister's three-year-old grandson climbed into her lap to find comfort. Snuggling close he said, "Grandma, my mommie makes me go to my room when I'm naughty."

"But, Jonathan, why are you naughty?" she asked, hugging him.

"Because I want to."

What honesty! Innocently, Jonathan centered in on his problem. He wanted *his* way. Often it is easier to blame our failures and sins on someone or something else rather than to admit our own responsibility and guilt. People have done that since the beginning of time. Adam blamed Eve and she blamed the serpent for their sin.

Not so with the tax-collector in Jesus' parable. The demeanor of the man says he knew he alone was responsible for his sin. As he prayed, he admitted he was not just a sinner but *the* sinner par excellence. There was no shifting of blame. And what was the result of putting the blame where it belonged? Jesus said the man was justified—forgiven.

Can we identify with the confession of the tax-gatherer? Do we honestly accept responsibility for our actions?

O God, forgive us when we try to squirm out of our guilt by rationalizing. Thank you that by your power we can be honest. Amen.

———————————

Take a moment to praise God and list times He's helped you face responsibilities:

———————————

151

... Reciprocating Love

Object Lesson

DONNA FLETCHER CROW

And be ye kind one to another, tenderhearted, forgiving one another, even as God for Christ's sake hath forgiven you. Ephesians 4:32, *KJV*

It was only a five-minute story. Simple, delicate, yet beautiful and profound. It always made me cry. I wanted to share it with my children.

"We don't want to hear it."

"It's stupid."

"Hurry up."

"Let's do something else."

I was hurt. Lord, what about the baby? Will she grow up to hurt my feelings, too? Can't I have one child who doesn't do that to me?

"No, my dear. Children always do that."

O Lord, I am your child. Do I sometimes hurt you in the same way?

He didn't say anything.

Please forgive me for the times you want to be

with me but I'm too busy; for the times I won't listen; for the times I prefer the company of my friends to the company of my heavenly Father.

"My child."

As you have commanded us to be kind and thoughtful to one another, help me also to be careful of my attitude toward you. As you give your love to me to share with others, help me also to return that love to you. Amen.

———————————

Take a moment to praise God and list times He's brought you back to Himself:

———————————

Grasping the Infinite

MARY LOU CARNEY

And the peace of God, which passeth all
understanding, shall keep your hearts and
minds through Christ Jesus.
Philippians 4:7, *KJV*

Arithmetic has never been my forte. I
have trouble visualizing the theories and denominations that delight my math-minded counterparts.
That's why I was pleased to see a huge aquarium in
the foyer of a school I visited recently. It was half-
filled with bottle caps. For months, staff and students
alike had been diligently collecting the caps, hoping
to fill the glass container with 10,000 of the ruffled
metal tops. Why? So the children could see what
10,000 of *something* looks like! I like that. It made
the huge number somehow more approachable, more
real.

I sometimes have trouble understanding the

things of God, too—things like His love, His patience, His peace. My finite mind stumbles at the miracle and magnitude of it all. But when my heart reaches out in simple faith to accept those wonders, yet another wonder occurs. The unseen, unfathomable things of God become *real.* I know His love; I witness His patience; I feel His peace. And, like those children watching the bottle caps accumulate, I begin to understand.

Thank you, God, for the wonder of all you are. Amen.

Take a moment to praise God and list ways you've experienced His wonder:

A Dandelion by Any Other Name... Could Be a Rose

MARGARET BROWNLEY

The smell of my son is as the smell of a field which the Lord hath blessed.
Genesis 27:27, *KJV*

It was May and the dandelions were back, just as they'd been for the past seven springs we'd lived in our house. We'd tried digging them up, poisoning them and even zapping them with an electrical device. Nothing deterred the pesky little weeds from plotting out a piece of ground and taking root. But on this particular spring day, our then two-year-old son Kevin taught us there was yet another way to battle dandelions.

It was Mother's Day and I was busy in the kitchen when I heard a small voice behind me.

"Happy Mudder's Day!"

I turned around and faced my son, who was beaming proudly. A bunch of dandelions were clenched in his chubby hands. He presented them to me as if they were the most precious gems in the world. I held the cluster of yellow flowers in my hands, my eyes moist. It had been the first real sign that my son had understood the concept of giving. My little guy was growing up.

Little did I know at the time what a lasting gift my son had bestowed on me. From then on, whenever I noticed the pesky little head of a dandelion, I would think back to that Mother's Day and find myself smiling. My son had unwittingly turned my less than perfect yard into a garden of "roses." Even now, years later, the warm memory of that day lingers like the fragrance of a summer bouquet.

Using the lesson our son taught us, we've managed to turn the many annoying "weeds" that have cropped up in our lives into roses. With a little work we were able to view a nosy neighbor in a more favorable light and concentrate on the security of knowing she was always on the job and that no stranger could possibly enter our neighborhood without her knowledge.

One "dandelion" in my life that I thought could never be turned into a rose is housework. But my husband proved me wrong one day when he impulsively wrote *I love you* in the dust on a neglected coffee table.

How easy it is to concentrate on the negative things in our lives. How much more rewarding it is to turn these pesky dandelions into roses. For as a rose fills a room with its fragrance, so will God's love fill our lives.

Dear God, let your love bloom within my heart so that I may make other lives more fragrant. Amen.

Mother Love
DIANTHA AIN

My mother lives within me,
   her love, her guiding hand,
   the wisdom she instilled
   when I could hardly understand.
She reminds me to be patient
   with myself and other folk,
   to stop and smell the flowers,
   to take the time to laugh and joke.
She gives me strength and courage
   to face adversities,
   and confidence and faith
   in my own abilities,
   reverence and devotion
   to a God she loved and knew.
He holds her for eternity.
   but she lives within me, too.

When Did Prejudice Creep In?

MARY BECKWITH

God is no respecter of persons.
Acts 10:34, *KJV*

It must be a gentlemanbug," I thought I heard my little boy say.

"What did you say?" I asked him.

He said it again. "It must be a gentlemanbug."

Rob, then Robbie, gently pushed the *lady*bug onto his pudgy little hand. He had been playing with it for at least 10 minutes. I was impressed that, at four years old, he knew the opposite for lady was gentleman and was able to label his new little friend accordingly.

But then I asked, "Why do you think it's a gentlemanbug?"

"Because he's smart!" was his ready reply.

Needless to say, I was in shock for a moment.

Where had he gotten the idea that, in order to be smart, you had to be a man? And at the age of four, at that!

I quickly tried to recall if, in the last few days, I had said something that would have implied men were smarter than women. I couldn't remember anything. Maybe his father had made that implication somehow. I'd have to ask him.

I do recall at times when the kids asked me questions I didn't have the answers to I'd say, "We'll ask Daddy when he gets home." Maybe I'd done it enough to give the impression that dads are smarter than moms.

Anyway, this little episode made me question, How does prejudice and bias enter our lives? What causes us to judge others because of gender or color or whatever? It also taught me that when we show partiality and prejudice, we are setting examples for our children.

I am so thankful we have a heavenly Father who is no respecter of persons. He loves each one of us the same. And He desires that we in turn love one another with the same kind of love.

When I'm reminded of His unconditional, steadfast love, it helps me fight against the prejudice that tries to creep in, distort my conception of others, and tempts me to look at myself more highly than I should.

Thank you, Jesus, that you came so that we might have life and have it more abundantly, all of us on an equal basis. Help us not to think of ourselves more highly than we should, and to love one another as you have loved us. Amen.

Crying Against the Kindergarten Door

LEONORE C. SCHUETZ

When she had said this, she went and called her sister Mary, saying quietly, "The Teacher is here and is calling for you."
John 11:28, *RSV*

As I walked toward my son, Gregory's, kindergarten room, I felt that the only thing holding me up was the soft touch of my children's hands. Though my two-year-old daughter's fingers radiated trust and my son's hand spoke of gentle love, my own heart was shrouded in grief. It had been only two days since my mother's funeral.

It was Gregory's second week of *big school* and he had eagerly accepted this new experience. However, this morning he didn't follow the line of children into the room. "Go on in, Gregory," I urged him.

161

He briskly walked away from me and headed for the gate.

"Gregory!"

He halted, eyeing me like a deer suspicious of an enemy.

Sensing that Gregory was having a delayed reaction to his grandma's funeral and my anguish, I approached him and calmly explained that he needed to go into the room. I assured him that his teacher had interesting things for him to do and learn.

Gregory let me nudge him inside the classroom. After I shut the door, I was dismayed when I heard him throw himself against it and burst into tears. My first impulse was to yank open the door and clutch my son in my arms. But I was stilled by the teacher's voice, which called reassuringly to him. Resolutely, I turned and walked away with my daughter.

I began to cry. The thought flooded in on me, *Haven't I been acting just like my son? I've been wailing at the kindergarten door for my mother to come back.*

When I got home, I knelt down and asked God to heal my broken heart and to fulfill my needs as He saw fit.

That night, I remembered how Jesus wept at the tomb of Lazarus. I thought it might comfort me to read the story again. As I did, I felt a spark of joy when Martha called Jesus "the Teacher." Happily, I realized Jesus is my ultimate Teacher—and my Comforter.

Dear Jesus, I look to you, my Teacher, for comfort and instruction this day. Amen.

. . . God's Mighty Power

Overwhelmed

RUTH M. BATHAUER

Great is the Lord and most worthy of praise.
Psalm 145:3, *NIV*

All week we had been talking about God, our Creator. As one of the teachers at a Christian camp for fourth and fifth graders, I'd had the joy of seeing their excitement as new truths about God dawned on them.

One of the last activities of a very busy, fun-filled day was our evening vespers. We hiked up to a grassy knoll where the campers flopped on the ground and began to sing some of their favorite songs; then it was time for our devotional thought. Surrounded by the beauty of nature and the wonders of God's handiwork, our attention was drawn to the first evening star twinkling in the twilight sky. We talked about the stars and agreed it was impossible to count them or even to see all of them with the naked eye. I read a psalm out loud that says God not only knows the number of stars but He has given a name to each one!

A great silence swept across the wiggling campers as that awesome thought registered. Suddenly, the silence was broken with, "Wow!"

I felt a lump swelling in my throat because I realized, in that one simple word, that child expressed the awe we all felt at that moment.

Have you been overwhelmed by the greatness of God recently? The Bible says God is omnipotent. No problem is too great for our all-powerful God. He is all-knowing and He knows our thoughts before we even express them! He is here with you and longs to communicate with you. What an amazing truth! Have you felt it? The psalmist did, and said:

> Great is the Lord and most worthy of
> praise . . . . He determines the number of
> the stars and calls them each by name.
> Great is our Lord and mighty in power;
> his understanding has no limit.
> Psalm 145:3; 147:4,5, NIV

Lord, we worship you in awe and wonder, for you are worthy of our praise. Amen.

... Facing Our Fears

Lions at Large

CAROL STEWART

*So the king gave the order, and they brought
Daniel and threw him into the lions' den. The
king said to Daniel, "May your God, whom you
serve continually, rescue you!"*
Daniel 6:16, *NIV*

It was my first day solo as the reading
teacher—the third teacher in four weeks—and the
kids were sizing me up. The class was made up of
seven junior high students with emotional and learning disabilities. They didn't handle change well, and I
wasn't particularly crazy about changes myself.

These are only kids, I reminded myself, but they
seemed as ferocious as the lions Daniel faced. Would
God be with me as He was with Daniel? My brain
said yes, but my heart still trembled.

The boundaries were drawn, class rules
explained, and the new situation assessed on both
sides of the line. The testing had begun—mine, not
theirs.

Mike put his feet on the desk and began pounding

his head on the room divider. "Mike, please stop that." No response. Oh well, ignoring him might be the best approach.

A spit wad zipped across the room, but I didn't see who sent it flying. "Miss Iverson wouldn't let that happen," Nora said. *I sure wish Miss Iverson were here!* I sighed to myself.

Steve began to laugh, while Travis sat perfectly still, an angelic innocence on his face. Then Jeff piped up, "Knock it off, you guys!" Another spit wad sailed by. The lesson was a shambles. No one was going to learn a thing about reading that day, I decided.

Mike began making squeaking noises. *At least he's not banging his head anymore!* I thought. *Dear God, how am I going to deal with all this?*

"Miss Iverson doesn't let Mike do that," Shawn informed me. I agreed. Mike shouldn't get away with his behavior, so I sent him to a time-out. Surprisingly enough, he went without comment.

Steve was losing control by then, and Joey was shrinking into his seat. Nora smirked. "Miss Iverson doesn't . . . " Shawn peeked around the corner at Mike and announced, "He's curled up inside the study carrel." "Miss Iverson wouldn't like that," Travis announced. *Oh, God, I think the lions are winning!*

Everyone rushed over to look at Mike. "Mike, you need to spend the rest of the period in the hall," I said as calmly as I could. He went out with a look of triumph. The other six began to look uncertain.

The perfect time for the *I-will-not-tolerate-this-behavior* lecture, I decided. The class was looking a bit sheepish, and silence prevailed at last. Was it the silence of defeat, or a retreat before a new attack? I glanced at the clock. Defeat or retreat, I must have been making progress—the lions were temporarily quiet, and Miss Iverson's name hadn't been mentioned for at least four minutes!

Help me, God, to face the lions in my life. I want to constantly serve you today no matter what the circumstances. Amen.

Take a moment to praise God and list fears He has helped you face:

. . . The Assurance of Truth

I Believe You!

MARY LOU CARNEY

In my Father's house are many mansions: if it were not so, I would have told you. I go to prepare a place for you. John 14:2, *KJV*

I was teaching school in Louisiana, and as October neared I felt especially homesick for my native Indiana with its fields of ripe corn and fat orange pumpkins. At Halloween, I looked forward to the arrival of carved, candle-lit jack-o'-lanterns on porches. To my dismay, the only pumpkins I saw were plastic! Inquiring at the local fruit market, I found out that pumpkins were not grown in the sandy soil of Louisiana and were, consequently, both scarce and costly.

The next day I told my fifth grade class about the pumpkin fields where I grew up—rows and rows of pumpkins as far as the eye could see. For a moment they were silent. Then someone in the back row laughed, "You expect us to believe that?" The rest of the room took it up, and my vision of pumpkin patches faded in the raucous incredulity of those children.

Later, at recess, one little boy approached me shyly. "I believe you," he whispered.

"Why?" I asked, intrigued at his singular faith when all his peers had doubted.

"Because . . . well, because I know you wouldn't lie to me."

Sometimes heaven seems far away; sometimes my arguments seem weak in the face of skeptics. How can I be sure? Because the One who told me is the Author of Truth—and He would never lie to me.

Thank you, Lord, for your loving preparation and quiet assurance. Amen.

Take a moment to praise God and list favorite truths from His Word:

Closed Mind, Closed Heart?

DONNA FLETCHER CROW

For the time will come when they will not stand wholesome teaching, but will follow their own fancy and gather a crowd of teachers to tickle their ears. They will stop their ears to the truth. 2 Timothy 4:3,4, *NEB*

My three-year-old daughter went through the room chanting a rhyme she'd learned at preschool: "(hands on mouth) If I close my mouth, I can't eat or talk; (hands over eyes) if I close my eyes, I can't see; (hands over ears) if I close my ears, I can't hear." She went happily on, her golden cocker puppy at her heels, but it left me thinking of the simple, yet profound truth she had spoken.

How often do I close myself off from the world around me—and from God? In my own mind, I finished her rhyme: "If I close my mind, I can't learn the truth; if I close my heart, I can't receive God's blessings."

O Lord, today help me to be open to the world of your creation, open to the people around me, and most of all, open to you.

Dear Father, open my eyes to the beauties of your creation, open my ears to the truth you speak, open my heart to your loving guidance. Amen.

Take a moment to praise God and list ways He's shown you to be open:

... Seeking His Guidance

My Special Child

DIANE REICHICK

Trust in the Lord with all your heart and lean not on your own understanding; in all your ways acknowledge him, and he will make your paths straight. Proverbs 3:5,6, *NIV*

God chose me to be the mother of a child with special needs. For 13 years, I worried about our son, and was determined to get to the root of his problems. Self-reliance, however, got me nowhere. Finally, I turned to God for help. That's when our miracle happened.

Aaron's educational handicaps were subtle at first, becoming more pronounced in elementary school. Behavioral problems and low achievement in relation to his potential led to exhaustive batteries of tests. The evaluations displayed borderline mental, physical and emotional problems with vague solutions. The problems, along with the continued testing, took their toll on Aaron.

When he was a third grader, we reluctantly made

the decision to place Aaron in a special class for the educationally handicapped. Aaron, who was severely overweight, became an ideal candidate for ridicule and teasing from his peers.

Aaron's self-esteem diminished daily. His frustrations were vented in anger and depression. There were times when he threatened to run away from home, and even talked of suicide. More and more, I began to wonder if it was something I had or hadn't done that had made Aaron the way he was.

And then, after turning the situation over to God and seeking His guidance, I took Aaron to a hematologist, instinctively requesting a complete blood test, concentrating on thyroid function. Contrary to the physician's professional opinion, the lab results indicated an extreme hypothyroid—or underactive thyroid—condition. I soon learned that the thyroid gland secretes the hormone thyroxine, which controls mental and physical growth and metabolism, which, in turn, affects behavior, emotions and school performance. Because the disease is initially symptom-free, it was possible that Aaron had been suffering from hypothyroidism since birth.

Only by the grace of God and through His direction was Aaron prevented from becoming permanently damaged in all areas of his life. Under the care of an endocrinologist, Aaron now has a new lease on life. Not only is he feeling and looking better, he has entered eighth grade with an improved attitude and a sense of self-worth for the first time.

Direct me, God, toward being the mother you want me to be. Amen.

Letters from Camp

MARGARET BROWNLEY

One day Jesus was praying in a certain place. When he finished, one of his disciples said to him, "Lord, teach us to pray." Luke 11:1, NIV

When my oldest son went away to summer camp for the first time, I was a nervous wreck. Although he was nine years old, he hadn't as much as spent a night away from home, let alone an entire week. I packed his suitcase with special care, making sure he had enough socks and underwear to see him through the week. I also packed stationery and stamps so he could write home.

I received the first letter from him three days after he'd left. I quickly tore open the envelope and stared at the childish scrawl, which read: *Camp is fun, but the food is yucky!*

The next letter offered little more: *Jerry wet the*

bed. Who's Jerry, I wondered. The third and last letter provided this interesting piece of news: *The nurse said it's not broken.*

Fragments. Bits of information that barely skim the surface. A preview of coming attractions that never materialize.

It made me think of my own sparse messages to God. "Dear Lord," I plead when a son is late coming home, "keep him safe."

"Give me strength," I pray when faced with a difficult neighbor or the challenge of a checkbook run amuck.

"Let me have wisdom," is another favorite prayer of mine, usually murmured in haste while waiting my turn at a parent/teacher conference or dealing with a difficult employee.

"Thank you, God," I say before each meal or when my brood is tucked in safely for the night.

Fragments. Bits and pieces. Are my messages to God as unsatisfactory to Him as my son's letters were to me?

With a guilty start, I realized that it had been a long time since I'd had a meaningful chat with the Lord.

When my son came home, he told me all about his adventures. It was good to have him back. I tucked him in bed that night and felt at peace. Although I knew that my son had been well cared for at camp and that I would have been notified had there been any serious problems, it was still comforting to hear firsthand that he was okay.

"Thank you, God," I murmured, and then caught myself. It was time I sent God more than just a hasty note from "camp."

Dear Father, help me to prioritize the countless things in my life that clamor for attention, so that I always have time for you. Amen.

Take a moment to praise God and list ways to improve your prayer life:

... The Need for Self-Confidence

I Don't Like Myself Today

BERIT KJOS

*I praise you because I am fearfully and
wonderfully made; your works are wonderful, I
know that full well.* Psalm 139:14, *NIV*

Mom, why do I always have to work
harder than the other kids?" Hot, tired and disturbed,
David burst into the house, full of questions.

"Why does it take longer for me to get my homework done than for Keith, and he gets better grades?
It isn't fair!" His serious blue eyes challenged me to
satisfy his sense of justice.

This wasn't the first time David had asked these
questions. They had been raised and answered again
and again. Intellectually, David knew the answers,
but today God's plan just didn't make sense.

I gazed at my youngest son. Under that tousled
blond hair were hidden many concerns.

What could I say to help build a sense of worth in my precious child? How could I help him see the sovereignty, wisdom and love of God who formed him with a planned set of strengths and weaknesses?

Feelings of helplessness surged through me. I longed to relieve David's frustration. Not having ready answers, I turned to my Lord who always does. Suddenly, the words began to flow.

"David, God has made you very special. You have a bright mind. You are fun to be with. You have a strong body . . . "

"But I'm no good in sports," David interrupted. "Last week I struck out three times. If I were good, I'd have more friends."

I put my arms around my son and held him close.

Looking up, I noticed the sign on the refrigerator: *God doesn't make junk.* A Scripture lit up in my mind.

"David, run and get your Bible. I want to read something with you."

Dutifully, David shuffled to his room and returned with a beat-up *NIV*. He handed it to me, and we sat down together.

"Psalm 139 has often encouraged me when I have felt inferior," I told David. "Here, read with me."

I read out loud while David whispered.

I praise you because I am fearfully and wonderfully made; your works are wonderful . . . .

"David, this doesn't answer all your questions, but it does remind us that God did a great job making you. Only He knows the future and how to prepare you. These struggles will make you strong in character—ready to meet the challenges ahead. Will you trust Him?"

David nodded, then smiled—and we hugged each other.

"Thank you, Lord, for winning the battle again," I whispered, as I put out the cookies and milk.

I know, my King, that your work and your ways are perfect. Thank you for the assurance, comfort, power and nearness of your Word. Amen.

———————

Take a moment to praise God and list personality traits He has given you:

Ask and Receive

KATHI MILLS

If you believe, you will receive whatever you ask for in prayer. Matthew 21:22, *NIV*

It was on a rare golden autumn day in the Pacific Northwest that my then two-year-old son, Chris, taught me the meaning of faith. I had taken him to the park for a picnic. As I unloaded the car, he ran on ahead, looking for the playground. Suddenly, I sensed that something was very wrong.

I dropped everything and began to run, praying for God's divine protection. Then I saw the slide. Chris had almost reached the top, climbing quickly and squealing with delight. Just as he got to the last rung he slipped, falling backward, headfirst, to the pavement below. Then, in that split second before he hit the ground, it was as if a cushion of feathers had been placed beneath him. He landed softly, bouncing up and looking at me quizzically, as if wondering why I was so upset.

I grabbed him and cried, "Chris, are you all right?"

He answered very simply, "Mom, the angels catched me." And off he went to play.

As I stood there, staring after my son, I wondered, Why am I so amazed? Why do I pray if I don't really believe God will answer?

And then I remembered an illustration I had once heard a pastor give about "believing prayers." It seems a woman was having doubts about what God could (or would) do in answer to prayer, so she decided to put Him to the test. She got down on her knees one night and began to pray, "God, if you can hear me, remove that tree outside my window!" On and on she prayed until, as the morning light came softly through the window, she arose and looked outside. "Aha!" she exclaimed. "Just as I thought! It's still there!"

I wonder how many of us are like that woman when we pray, mouthing the words, but not really expecting an answer. Oh, I know His answer won't always be yes, but He does hear, He does care, and—as I humbly learned from a two-year-old—He always answers believing prayers.

Lord, teach us to pray with the unquestioning faith of a child. Amen.

... His Miracle of Love

A Crooked Paper Heart

ADREW ROGERS SLYDER

Therefore, whoever humbles himself like this child is the greatest in the kingdom of heaven.
Matthew 18:4, *NIV*

It is my habit early each morning to walk outside and look around the front yard. One day recently, I woke up feeling burdened and depressed. I don't know what I expected to find as I slowly shuffled toward the front door and looked outside but, as I peered out into the bright morning sunshine, I found a miracle.

It was in the shape of a little pink paper heart, obviously cut out by small hands and stuck low on the front door with tape. *Now, who do you suppose . . . ?* I asked myself, a smile tugging at the corners of my mouth.

Could it be the little girl next door? I wondered,

gazing tenderly at the lopsided heart. *No, she's too old. She would have cut a perfect heart. And Matthew—no, it couldn't be* Matthew. He's too young . . . .

As I reached out and carefully removed the little pink heart from my front door, I felt as if a mountain of doubt and frustration had been removed from within. I walked back into the house and closed the door behind me, cradling my paper heart gently in my hand. *Who, Lord? Who could have put it there? And why?*

I later learned that it had indeed been little Matthew—only four years old—who had cut out the little heart and taped it to my front door. Apparently, his Sunday School teacher had enlisted her class in the GSS (God's Secret Service), and their mission was to do something special for someone by leaving a pink paper heart to show that it was a gift of love. And they were not to tell who had done the good deed.

What had I done to deserve the pink heart? Absolutely nothing, so far as I could tell. And what about Matthew? Why had he chosen to put the heart on my door? I don't suppose I'll ever know. That's Matthew's secret.

For me, it was so much more than a lopsided pink paper heart or a good deed done by a small child. It was a miracle that lightened my load that day—a miracle of love.

Father, as a little child, teach me to be trusting and open to being used by you to give someone else a miracle. Amen.

I Should Have Known by Now

JANET BLY

Do not let your hearts be troubled. Trust in
God; trust also in me. John 14:1, *NIV*

I had no time to worry about a small boy's moods that Saturday morning. While our seven-year-old fussed and whined with his friends over the TV video games, I stewed over my own mounting pile of pressures.

A stack of several hundred pieces of potential church choir anthems teetered in the corner, waiting to be reviewed. A dozen important phone calls I needed to make before noon all produced busy signals. A week's worth of laundry spilled out into the garage. A letter with some upsetting news was spread out on the kitchen table. A half-finished grocery list for ten Sunday lunch guests decorated the refrigerator door.

In the midst of this turmoil, Aaron's Sunday School teacher called. "Is Aaron going to Chuck E. Cheese with us today?"

"I . . . I'm sorry," I stuttered. "He didn't mention anything about a trip to a pizza parlor . . . . "

"Well, we'll be leaving about three. If he didn't bring home a permission slip, just write the usual information on a slip of paper and send it along with him."

As soon as I reminded Aaron about the party, he danced around in anticipation for the rest of the day. Then, just as I pulled a carrot cake out of the oven for Sunday's lunch, the doorbell rang. A minute later, I heard a commotion.

Rushing to the front door, I found two neighbor girls waving pink papers at Aaron, who was hiding behind the drapes, sobbing.

Gently, I pulled him out and coaxed him to talk to me.

"I can't go!" he wailed.

"What do you mean?"

"I don't have one of those pink papers!"

"Oh, yes, you do. Yours just happens to be white. I've got it all taken care of." I wiped his tears, folded the signed release paper into his pocket, and sent him off.

Back in the kitchen, I mulled the scene over in my mind again. Why hadn't he just asked me about the paper? Hadn't he been my child long enough to know I'd have a solution?

And then, at that very moment, it seemed I heard a soft echo right beside me—my own words repeated with the hint of a smile. *Haven't you been my child long enough to know I have it all taken care of?*

Quietly, I made my way through the house. I stopped for a moment beside the stacks of music, the load of clothes, the troublesome letter, and released each one to the care of my heavenly Father.

Father God, by an act of my will, I refuse to allow my heart to be troubled about these cares of the world. Help me find the solution you've already provided. Amen.

———————————————

Take a moment to praise God and list everyday needs He's supplied:

Take
A
MOMENT
A
DAY

to learn about God . . .

. . . In Giving to Others
We Learn About . . .

Seasoned Gifts

JANET BLY

*Even in old age they will still produce fruit and
be vital and green. This honors the Lord, and
exhibits his faithful care.* Psalm 92:14,15, *TLB*

We'd just heard a series of sermons on all the varieties of spiritual gifts. As I walked out of the sanctuary, my mind buzzed with ministry possibilities I could hardly wait to begin. First, I'd start that women's Bible study I'd been considering. Then, I'd write up a draft of a weekly youth program idea . . . .

Mildred, an elderly friend, passed me in the hall just then, and I greeted her, then hurried over to the church nursery. While I gathered up story papers and sweaters, and shook out cracker crumbs for my two sons, my mind wandered back to Mildred. *She didn't seem her usual perky self,* I mused. *I wonder if something's wrong?*

The boys and their belongings tucked into the station wagon, I ran back to find Mildred.

"How are you really doing today?" I asked her.

She clutched my arm in appreciation. "Oh, I'm

doing just fine, thank you. Only .. "

"Only, what?"

Her eyes searched mine. "You're young, active, able to do things—I sure don't begrudge you that— but, you know, I still have just as strong a desire to serve God as I ever did. Only difference is, there's nothing I can do—is there?"

"Oh, sure there is!" I answered, but I couldn't think of a single thing at the moment. I promised to pray about it.

Several months passed and nothing more was said. But then, one day, I got a call from Mildred.

"Say, Janet, do you know where I can find a good supply of Christian storybooks?"

Her words spilled out with growing excitement. "You know those children I've complained about in that new apartment building behind my house? The ones always running through my garden and making so much noise? Well, a week ago Monday, several of them were playing in my front yard. I decided to pull a chair out on the grass where they were and read awhile. Before I knew it, all three of them sat quiet as can be beside me while I read out loud."

She paused to catch her breath. "You know what? They've been coming back every afternoon and bringing their friends. Today I had a dozen of them! But now I've run out of suitable books."

We rejoiced together at the Lord's provision of an unexpected ministry opportunity right outside her own front door.

Father, I praise you for your loving creativity, which brings so many surprises, no matter what our age or circumstances. Amen.

190

A Beacon of Light

SUSAN F. TITUS

Shine out among them like beacon lights,
holding out to them the Word of Life.
Philippians 2:15,16, *TLB*

As the fog rolled in, the damp air chilled me. Shivering, I zipped my blue windbreaker tightly around my neck. I walked faster, hoping an increased heart rate would mean greater warmth to my body. In spite of the darkness, I was determined to take my nightly walk along the shore. This was my quiet time.

The clouds overhead blocked the moon, so I carefully picked my way across the rocky portion of the beach to the sandy stretch. In the distance, I saw the beacon from the lighthouse on the point. I used its flashing light to guide me.

As a wife, mother and member of the working force, I often felt many demands on my time. I watched the circling light in the distance and thought of how often my life revolved like that beacon, going nowhere. All my busy activities suddenly seemed insignificant.

And yet, that lamp guided all the passing ships in the night. The captains didn't crash or sail too near the shore because of one bright light.

As I continued to watch the revolving beacon, I felt a close identity with the light. Perhaps I, too, could shine, revealing God's Word at work in me. Many of my co-workers were not Christians. Sometimes, they asked my advice. Perhaps I might influence their lives more if I set an example of a loving, joyful Christian. Instead of preaching at them, I could listen to them.

And what about my children? Instead of tuning them out while driving to their after-school activities, I'd use those precious moments. The conversation could be channeled to draw our family closer together and nearer to God. I would concentrate on listening to my children.

Finally, I reached the lighthouse on my nightly walk. It was time to turn around and go home, but I lingered for a moment, gazing at the powerful light. Tomorrow I would try to imitate that lamp, shining brightly to help those who crossed my path.

Dear Lord, help me to reach out to those around me with your love. Please allow me to be a beacon of your light. Amen.

. . . Relaxed Availability

Keep It Simple!
DORIS W. GREIG

*My God shall supply all your needs according
to His riches in glory in Christ Jesus.*
Philippians 4:19, *NASB*

One summer, we had visited in many
churches in Mexico, and everywhere we went my
husband would say, "If you are ever up our way, do
come and see us."

Well, one summer day at about 3:30 in the afternoon, the doorbell rang. It was very hot that day, and
I had been lifeguarding by the pool. I ran to the door
and opened it to a group of five teachers and a pastor I
vaguely remembered meeting in Mexico.

Beyond them across the street, I saw two buses,
each packed with about 20 junior- and senior-high
school students. They were on a singing tour for the
Lord, and their next stop was Glendale. So, they had
all come to see us!

Remember the K.I.S.S. motto: "Keep it simple,

stupid!'"? Well, that's just what I did. While everyone came in, changed into bathing suits and went for a swim, I got wieners and buns out of the freezer, and someone else went to the store for fruit and ice cream. We used paper plates and fed everyone, while sitting around the pool. We all had such a good time.

Now, had I known earlier about this gang coming, I would really have panicked! Looking back, I'm glad I did the meal simply, so I too could enjoy the teachers and young people. God provided everything just when I needed it.

I don't know who wrote it, but I love this little poem:

If you have faith—God's got the power!

If you make the commitment—God opens the way!

If you make the pledge—God gives you the winning edge!

Thank you, Lord, for those little surprises along the way to show hospitality, even when it isn't convenient. And thank you for supplying everything we need just when we need it! Amen.

Adapted from *We Didn't Know They Were Angels* by Doris W. Greig. © Copyright by Doris W. Greig 1987. Published by Regal Books, Ventura, CA. Used by permission.

Success or Failure?

MARIETTA GRAMCKOW

Likewise, I say unto you, there is joy in the presence of the angels of God over one sinner that repenteth. Luke 15:10, KJV

One day, several years ago, I felt the Lord wanted me to start a neighborhood Bible study for children. Nervous and uncertain, with visions of a house full of noisy, excited youngsters, I extended an open invitation, purchased my teaching materials, prepared the lessons—and prayed.

The day of the first weekly Bible study arrived and I eagerly waited for the children. Finally, at 3:30 in the afternoon, two young boys rang the doorbell. I invited them in and talked to them about Jesus. Neither boy had ever been to church, and they both came from broken homes. They showed an interest in the lesson, and things seemed to go well.

The second week, however, only one boy returned. He had many questions, which I answered from the Bible. Finally, I asked him if he would like to ask Jesus to be his Savior, and he replied that he really would. We prayed together and he asked Jesus into his heart. Happy and excited, he hurried home to tell his mother the good news.

"I'll see you next week!" he called as he ran out the door.

But the next week, no one came for Bible study. The following two weeks were the same. I prayed and waited, then decided to call the mother of the little boy who had prayed and accepted Jesus. How disappointed I was to learn that he had moved back to town to live with his father! Then I asked his mother if her son had told her about asking Jesus to be his Savior. She replied that he had, and that she was glad for him. But when I tried to talk to her about doing the same, she said, "Perhaps some other time." She has since moved away.

I had been so sure God wanted me to start that Bible study! I had planned and prayed, but it all seemed to fall apart. And then the Lord reminded me that I had not failed at all. A young boy had come to know Jesus. God's purposes had been accomplished, and I rejoiced in that.

Father, help us not to base our success on numbers, but to concentrate on being obedient to you. Amen.

. . . Giving Our Best

The Best Gift

LINDA ALEAHMAD

*So let each one give as he purposes in his
heart, not grudgingly or of necessity; for God
loves a cheerful giver.* 2 Corinthians 9:7, KJV

The best things come in small packages," I had often been told as a child. So it was no surprise that the Brownie Christmas party found me greedily eyeing the tiniest package on the gift table.

No matter if Lindsey took a large box wrapped in metallic red paper, or if Sally got the Jane Russell paper dolls—the tiny package in green wrapping was still there waiting for me.

It was my turn. I approached the table, my Buster Brown haircut as neat as my Brownie uniform was messy. The littlest gift was mine! What wondrous gem was waiting within? I eagerly tore open the package to find—domino barrettes.

I fought back the tears. So much for the best things being in small packages.

197

A week later, I passed on the barrettes at the Sunday School gift exchange. By now I was wise in the ways of gift selections. My newfound wisdom brought me just the gift I wanted—stationery, my secret passion.

Clutching my gift at my side, I wandered about the room, listening to squeals of delight as other children opened their gifts.

"What did you get?" I quizzed my friend Nancy who looked none too happy.

"I got a dumb gift," she moaned. "I got domino barrettes!"

I was suddenly stunned to realize my gift—given with such selfish intentions—had caused my best friend pain.

It was then that I first began to grasp the true meaning of giving. As I stood there in that Sunday School class so many years ago, God—who loved me so much He sent His only Son to die for me—showed me that, when you give, you give your very best. As He did.

Lord, thank you for your priceless gift at Calvary. Help me to remember that a gift from me is an extension of myself, a reaching out to touch another, and remind me to give in the spirit of love—for as I give, so shall I receive. Amen.

. . . Developing Our Creativity

The Faith of a Dreamer

DIANTHA AIN

And a little child shall lead them.
Isaiah 11:6, *KJV*

Starting a new career is a scary proposition at any age. But I decided, after 30 years of being a helpmate and homemaker, that I wanted to be a writer and songwriter. So I overlooked the terror clutching my heart and signed up for a writing course. At that point, I didn't even know for sure what I wanted to write.

How was I to know which path to choose? What I enjoyed writing was poetry, but all the *experts* were advising against that. The children's stories I was assigned were a pleasant challenge, but definitely not what I wanted to write on a regular basis. I prayed for guidance and waited.

Between assignments, I wrote what I wanted to write, mostly verse. As a little girl, I always enjoyed reciting poems and singing songs. I liked pretending and play-acting. Times may have changed, but I couldn't believe children didn't still enjoy those same things.

It had been a long time since my children were small, so I took my poems to a friend who teaches kindergarten. She could tell me if I was on the right track.

"I think you should write about 20 of them," she casually remarked.

Wow! That's 16 more! I silently calculated. *I wonder if I can?*

Panic reared up in my stomach, but I feigned a calm reply. "Okay, I'll see what I can do."

With the next batch of poems, I showed her some sketches I had done. She encouraged me to attempt my own illustrations. In two months, I accumulated 30 poems and 19 illustrations. Then she invited me to share them with her class. When she saw the children's reaction, she asked me to come back on a weekly basis, and she suggested I write some special songs.

That's how I began cultivating creativity in children. Since its inception in 1981, my program has introduced over 6,000 youngsters to the joys of poetry, music and pantomime. My new career is the most exciting, rewarding work I have ever done.

Thanks to the *little girl* in me, many other children are reaping benefits. My prayer has been answered in a way I never could have expected.

And my *little girl* is happier now than she ever was when I was her age.

Dear Lord, may I always be open to share the gifts you've given me in the way only you know best. Amen.

... Extending Hospitality

Transferred!

CAROL STEWART

Share with God's people who are in need.
Practice hospitality. Romans 12:13, *NIV*

Transferred! A new job in another building—and I don't know anyone there. As I walk through the halls with a tentative smile on my face, my thoughts trail me like a dark, heavy cloud.

So many new faces, and such a long time to match them up with names! Oh, there's Bessie and Miguel—and Carol. I think she's unhappy I've been bumped into Jennifer's job. It wasn't the way I'd planned it, either! I hope Jennifer finds a new job quickly.

Good, here's the office. Doris, Iris and Idell always have a ready smile and a friendly word. What would we do without the secretaries who really run the place?

I dread going into the lunch room. The same people always seem to sit together, and I don't know any of the *in* jokes! There's a party tonight at Bruce's house. I don't really want to go, but I don't want to be left out, either. Everyone seems to be talking about it.

Should I sit by myself or sit with that group? What if they don't want me? Guess I'll sit over here. I hope someone will come sit by me. Maybe they're as uncomfortable with this situation as I am!

In a spot where I am ill at ease and not in control, I need someone to say, "It's good you're here," instead of looking at me as though I'm being sized up and placed into preconceived ideas of what my niche will or should be. I know I don't look or do things like Jennifer, but if the atmosphere is open, friendly and kind, you may find out more quickly that you like me, even if I am different. I can't take anyone's place, but I need the space to make my own place.

Being in need of hospitality myself, I realize how much I need to practice it with others.

Dear God, help me practice hospitality to the people I meet. I choose to practice an attitude of openness and acceptance at home, at work and in the community today. Amen.

. . . Courage to Get Involved

Can You Walk Your Talk?

LINDA MONTOYA

Train a child in the way he should go, and when he is old he will not turn from it.
Proverbs 22:6, *NIV*

Why do people drink and drive?" asked my eight-year-old daughter, Melanie, as we sat outside a fast-food restaurant. Her questions on the subject continued, and it became obvious that she was deeply concerned about drunk drivers. Even after we discussed the issue, her anxiety continued, so I said, "Melanie, we need to pray." I closed my eyes and said, "Father, please protect our family from ever being harmed by a drunk driver. And, Lord, if I ever see someone drinking and driving, give me the courage to get involved. Amen."

Moments later, we stopped at a pizza place to pick up my teenage daughter. A boy of about 16 parked his car next to ours. Then he took a swig from a bottle of beer. *Lord, is this a test?* I wondered.

Melanie looked over at him just as he took a second drink of beer. Her brown eyes opened wide. Then she looked at me and said simply, "Well?"

As I hesitated, she went on. "Courage, Mom? Is that what you prayed for? And not even five minutes ago! What are you going to do?"

I wasn't sure as I glanced again at the nice looking boy. Silently, I prayed, "Lord, if you can get my feet out the door, I'll do it."

Taking a deep breath, I got out of the car and approached him. "Excuse me," I said. "I saw you drinking a beer."

"No," he replied nervously. "It's just a soda."

"May I see it?"

"No," he answered. After a moment of silence, he looked up at me and asked, "What do you want?"

"I don't want you to drink and drive."

His tone was polite, his question, challenging. "So, what are you going to do?"

"I have to do something," I explained. "I have no choice." And then I told him the whole story of Melanie's concern and my prayers about getting involved.

Calmly, he replied, "Do you want me to get rid of it?"

"If you throw it away, I won't report you," I assured him.

Our eyes met briefly. Then he opened the door, got out of the car, and tossed the bottle into a nearby trash can. As he walked back toward me, he smiled. "Thanks for caring about me," he said softly.

Swallowing the lump in my throat, I climbed back into the car beside my daughter.

Lord, give me the courage to live out the principles I preach to my children. Amen.

The Kind of Friend I Want to Be

DORIS W. GREIG

Greater love has no one than this, that one lay down his life for his friends.
John 15:13, *NASB*

As I think about friendship, I wonder if I had my life to live over, how differently I would live it.

Would I have invited more friends over for dinner, even if it were just for a hamburger fry or macaroni and cheese? Would I have sat on the lawn more often with my neighbors and visited while we watched the children play?

Would I have cried more often with them when appropriate, and laughed more often when that was in order? Would I have said, "I'm sorry," more often?

I want to be more like the kind of friend found in this acrostic:

F—Fun loving; Feeling of acceptance; Faithful

R—Risk being real, understood, even misunderstood

I—Interested in the welfare of others; Impartial

E—Expect the best of others; Empathetic

N—Natural relationship, a wholesome acceptance of others; Non-exclusive

D—Diplomatic; Delightful to be with; Durable in hard times

S—Sympathetic; Supportive with prayer and help; Stable

H—Helpful; Hopeful; Healing; Happy

I—Interdependent by helping others

P—Patient; Protective of reputation and confidences; Pleasant to be with; Personable

If I were given another opportunity at life and friendship, I would seize every minute of it! I would look at it and really see it and live it for Jesus.

Thank you, Father, for the friends you've brought into my life. Please remind me to live each day knowing I will never live this day again and help me to be the kind of friend I would like my friends to be. Amen.

Adapted from *We Didn't Know They Were Angels* by Doris W. Greig. © Copyright by Doris W. Greig 1987. Published by Regal Books, Ventura, CA. Used by permission.

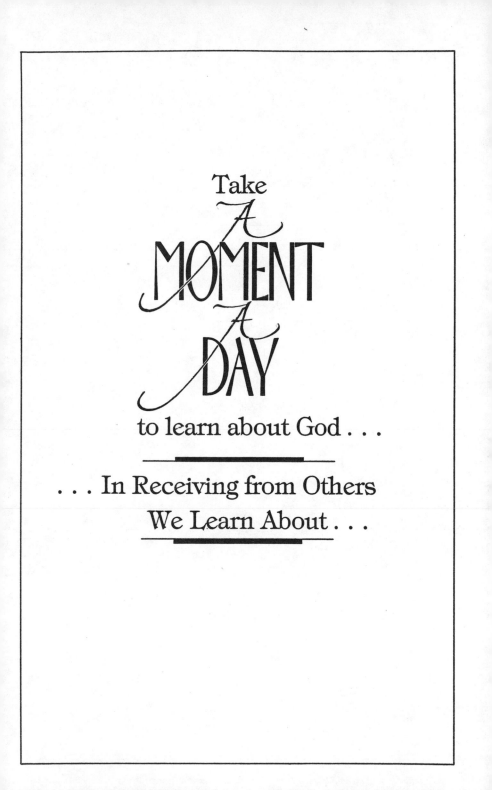

Take

A

MOMENT

A

DAY

to learn about God . . .

. . . In Receiving from Others
We Learn About . . .

... Unconditional Love

Blue-Ribbon Mentality

JUNE CURTIS

Dwell on the fine, good things in others.
Philippians 4:8, *TLB*

One of our family's favorite activities is attending the County Fair every August. The rides, food and exhibits are fun, interesting and, on occasion, learning experiences. We particularly enjoy examining the animals so proudly displayed by their owners.

Each animal is judged according to certain criteria, such as general appearance, quality of fur, stature, color, development of physique, etc., and then awarded blue, red or white ribbons accordingly.

I had no idea how often we use our own criteria to judge others—awarding them with blue ribbons, red or white ribbons, or possibly no ribbons at all—until, while driving down the freeway one day, I was taught an unforgettable lesson about unconditional love and acceptance.

I was returning home from a speaking engagement when, suddenly, a car came hurtling around the corner, became airborne, and flew over the outside guard rail out of sight. I only had time to pray, "God, protect that person, please!"

I stopped and ran to see where the car had landed. It was resting on its wheels approximately 150 feet below. As I started down to help, I could see the driver—a woman—still sitting behind the steering wheel. The descent was difficult, as it was raining and the ground was mud and rock. When I arrived, shoeless and drenched, I opened the car door, but the woman pushed past me and started running. Then, shock took over, and she fell into a pool of water.

Two men and a policeman arrived as I prayed and praised the Lord aloud for sparing the woman's life. As we waited for an ambulance, I held her head in my lap. She was of another race, had no teeth, was dirty, and smelled strongly of alcohol. But as the love of Jesus Christ flowed through me, she became a blue-ribbon winner. Such love is divine, not human. I admit to having certain biases. I like cleanliness, and abhor liquor, but those factors became unimportant as God loved her through me.

I began to tell her about God—the object of her swear words—about how much He loved her.

She answered emphatically, "No one has ever loved me!"

"You're wrong," I insisted. "God loves you, and so do I." I meant it.

As she was placed in the ambulance, she sat up on the stretcher and threw her arms around me. She began sobbing and crying, "Don't leave me, please, don't leave me!" For the first time in her life, she had felt love—not my love, but God's love, flowing toward her through a very improbable instrument—me.

Lord, remove the judgmental barriers that often prevent us from being channels of your love toward others. Amen.

God's Gift
DIANTHA AIN

God is love, and love is God;
Yet each of us may share.
His power dwells within us,
To nurture and to care.
We generate His energy
By giving it away.
So, love and live and freely give . . .
Give of yourself each day.

The "Little Woman"

DALE EVANS ROGERS

Yet who knows whether you have come to the kingdom for such a time as this?
Esther 4:14, *NKJV*

Some females detest being called "the little woman." I was one of those years ago. Have you ever thought how mighty the influence of the "little woman" can be?

Remember Esther in the Bible? She was a woman whose clear judgment and intelligence matched her beauty. Here was a simple Hebrew woman who was chosen to be queen of the greatest empire on earth at that time, the Kingdom of Persia. She discovered that intrigue was rampant in the court and that Haman, a favorite of the king, was hatching a plan to kill all the Jews. Haman was the Hitler of the Old Testament.

Queen Esther, risking her own life, revealed the

plot of Haman to her husband, the king, and saved her people from certain disaster.

Esther exerted her woman power as the woman behind the throne. If she had lived today, she probably would have tried to initiate a *coup d'etat* and taken over the throne herself!

Roy and I were in London to appear on the popular "Muppet Show." We were getting a little exercise between rehearsals by taking a brisk walk up the Strand. We passed a young Japanese couple, and I noticed that the man was walking quite a bit ahead of the woman, as is the custom in some countries. She was not in the least perturbed, but serenely smiling.

I have never particularly cottoned to this tradition. In fact, I found myself bristling at the sight. However, after considering the astounding divorce rate in America (in comparison with that of Japan), my bristles started to subside. If a woman is content to walk behind her man, why incite her to dissatisfaction? We are not all temperamentally alike. What an incredibly dull world this would be otherwise! God has gifted each of us as He sees fit. Some of us may not relish the idea of taking a backseat to a man in any area. On the other hand, all the seats cannot be front ones, can they? We should remember that the winds of adversity hit harder at the front seat.

Thank you, God, for making me a truly liberated woman in your service. Amen.

Adapted from *Woman Be All You Can Be* by Dale Evans Rogers with Carole C. Carlson. Copyright © 1980 by Dale Evans Rogers (Old Tappan, NJ: Fleming H. Revell Company; London: Hodder & Stoughton Ltd). Used by permission.

. . . The Importance of Encouragement

Gravity at Work

SHARON MAHOE

Therefore encourage one another, and build up one another, just as you also are doing.
1 Thessalonians 5:11, *NASB*

The tears rolled out of my eyes and down into my ears. I was lying on my back, you see. Gravity was at work. (The other kind of gravity was at work, too. Nothing was funny. Nothing at all.)

I reached for my Bible. It fell open (honest) at Lamentations. Through blurring tears I read verse 17, chapter 3: *I have been deprived of peace; I have forgotten what prosperity is (NIV).* (Things did seem bad.) *Yet, this I call to mind and therefore I have hope: Because of the Lord's great love we are not consumed, for his compassions never fail* (vv. 21,22).

So many times in those past few weeks I had come home to hear a message of encouragement on my answering machine: "Thinking of you"; "I love you"; even a couple of "Who loves ya, baby?"

What does a supposedly self-sufficient person like me have to go through before I can know how deep is the caring of my friends? A lot! Day after day, when hysteria and raw emotions were my constant companions during my divorce, I found the incredible support and concern of friends every time I needed someone. (Sometimes, even when I thought I didn't.)

On one of those particularly fragile days, I came into my office to find a large rectangular box on my desk. Mystified, I opened it to find—carefully arranged amidst hills of white tissue—fragrant soaps, shampoo, lotions and bubble bath. The note said, "For the times when things get bad. When you use these I'm thinking of you. I love you, Kathleen."

Kathleen Mary. Her dear gesture that day gave me peace in the midst of swirling clouds of panic. Each bubble bath, every time I smelled the fragrant soaps on my skin, I felt her love and concern for me. She gave me a token of her support and encouragement, the warmth of which has lasted for years.

Encouragement has never filled a flat tire. Encouragement has never made a car payment, nor fixed a broken washing machine. But encouragement from another gives us the strength to do what we feel we cannot do, hold on when we feel we cannot hold on, and try what we might not dare to try.

Encouragement. Doesn't sound like much, but it's everything. Spend some encouragement today. You'll be part of someone's memories for a long, long time.

Lord, open my eyes and my heart to see someone I may encourage by a few words, a hug, a loving gesture, or just something to make them laugh, then get up and try again. Amen.

... Failing Successfully

Feasting on the Slopes

JILL BRISCOE

The Lord is close to the brokenhearted and saves those who are crushed in spirit.
Psalm 34:18, *NIV*

A friend stopped in to see me this week. She surprised me with her visit and asked me what I was doing. I told her I was writing a book called *How to Fail Successfully.* She laughed at the title and then said, "If you want any tips give me a call. I'm 'between failures' at the moment, and life is good, but I've felt the heartbeat of God in the last few months—He has been *that* close to me!" Turning to go, she added, "If all that blessing can come out of an experience of failure, than I'm ready to fail again."

I knew she had lost her husband, and had fallen apart for a few weeks. She felt she had failed to give a testimony during her grief. Lying in His arms, with her leg broken with the rod of bereavement, she experienced the love of God in her valley of death, and stopped blaming herself for her lack of faith. "He wanted to teach me to lie still until I was healed," she said. "What a relief to realize He didn't expect me to do anything else but rest. He's carried me right through that whole adjustment period, and here I am on the slopes again."

I noticed she didn't say mountaintop—for who ever is found on the mountaintop when half of you has been taken away? But I watched her on the slopes feasting with God and I worshiped.

Father, thank you for being near to us when all else seems to have fallen apart. Thank you for bringing healing out of brokenness. Amen.

Adapted from *How to Follow the Shepherd . . . When You're Being Pushed Around by the Sheep* by Jill Briscoe. © Copyright 1982 by Jill Briscoe. Published by Fleming H. Revell Company. Used by permission.

No Shortcuts to Being Faithful

NICOLE HILL

He makes them listen to correction and
commands them to repent of their evil.
Job 36:10, *NIV*

Last spring, my husband and I had our income tax returns done. I was extremely busy with all of the usual activities of life at the time, and hurriedly ran about pulling open drawers, looking for records and receipts, all about an hour before I was supposed to have the information gathered together. I *guesstimated* how much we had donated for charities and how much we had put out for medical expenses. Maurie, our good-natured accountant, made a few jokes about my haphazard record keeping. I began to feel uncomfortable, but silently reasoned that I had done all I was able under the circumstances.

The next morning, as I left the house for my Bible

study, I murmured a quick prayer. "Lord, I feel uneasy about yesterday. If you want me to go back through all my records and do it right, I will. Just let me know."

On the way to the Bible study, the woman who was driving began to talk about being a Christian and being obedient to the Lord even in small things. She spoke about how her mother laughs at her for returning change at the market when she has received too much. And then she said her mother laughs at her for being so scrupulously honest on her income tax!

I squirmed in my seat, my face flushing red. I knew what I had to do. Although it was slightly embarrassing to call our accountant back with the correct figures, I felt better once I had. And I felt a whole lot better knowing that I had been obedient to the Lord's voice.

Dear Lord, help me to be faithful to you in all things. Amen.

Take a moment to praise God and list times you've obeyed His promptings:

... The Power of
Intercessory Prayer

Standing in the Gap

KATHI MILLS

*I looked for a man among them who would
build up the wall and stand before me in the
gap.* Ezekiel 22:30, *NIV*

Looking back on my life prior to my conversion in 1974, I realize now there were many intercessors on my behalf. In addition to my own dear family who prayed for me faithfully, I remember one instance in particular when God burdened the heart of a woman I hardly knew to pray for me.

I was in a hospital, far from home and family, drifting in and out of consciousness. Several times I became aware of a woman's voice praying for my salvation, as well as for my physical healing. At one point I heard a doctor describing my condition as critical, warning that I might not survive.

It was then that I recognized the voice of my intercessor once again as she spoke out in faith, "Doctor, I respect what you say, but I cannot accept it. I've been praying for Kathi and I believe she will not only recover, she will walk out of here and live for God someday!"

Before long, I did walk out of that hospital, returned to work, and learned that it was my boss's wife (I had only met her twice) who had "stood in the gap" for me. When I tried to thank her, she responded with a confident smile, "Don't thank me—thank God! He has great plans for your life."

Soon after that I moved away, never to see her again; but five year later when I gave my life to Christ, I remembered her—this faithful woman of God who never saw the results of her prayers for my salvation, but who believed God to answer those prayers *in His time.*

Lord, make us willing to stand in the gap for others. Amen.

———————

Take a moment to praise God and list intercessors in your life:

———————

. . . Looking Beyond the Obvious

Mall Madness

MARGARET BROWNLEY

In thy light shall we see light. Psalm 36:9, *KJV*

As soon as we turned into the parking lot, I knew we were crazy. It was two weeks before Christmas and I still had the inevitable last-minute shopping to do, but to agree to go to the largest shopping mall for miles—on a Saturday afternoon—was sheer madness.

I turned to my friend Connie. "Are you sure you want to go through with this?"

Connie, who had spotted a parking space, looked like she'd just won the lottery. Obviously, she wasn't thinking clearly.

"It'll be okay," she said with a bright smile.

As predicted, the stores were mobbed. "Jingle Bell Rock" blared from hidden speakers and irritable mothers scolded cranky toddlers. I was ready to quit before we'd begun.

"What does any of this have to do with Christmas?" I cried out in dismay.

"Everything!" Connie replied, much to my surprise. "This is exactly how it was on that first Christmas in Bethlehem."

For a moment I was taken aback. I'd always envisioned that first Christmas as the serene, peaceful one so often pictured on Christmas cards. But, of course, it hadn't been like that at all. One can well imagine the mood that must have prevailed among the travelers who, after coming long distances, had to fight crowds and face the lack of accommodations just to take part in a nose count!

Yet, it was in this mall-like atmosphere that God chose to present His most precious gift to the world. It was in this unlikely setting that the Christ child was born. With this thought in mind, I was amazed at the treasures we discovered during the remainder of the day.

We saw a stranger step forward to help a young girl whose money didn't cover the cost of her mother's gift. We heard a boy in a wheelchair ask Santa to bring a puppy for his sister. We smiled at two lovers who stood wistfully looking at diamonds and spinning dreams for the future. Connie was right. That crowded mall had everything to do with Christmas.

Lord, forgive my blindness. Help me to open my eyes so that I can look beyond crowded malls and into the Kingdom of God. Amen.

... Healing Through Interaction

Taking a Chance

CAROL BECKERDITE

Little children, let us not love with word or with tongue, but in deed and truth. We shall know by this that we are of the truth, and shall assure our heart before Him.
1 John 3:18,19, *NASB*

Years ago, when I first joined the church I now attend, I knew only a few people there. I felt isolated and out of the mainstream, especially as a` young widow. Another single parent about my own age consistently made attempts at being friendly. At first, it bothered me. Part of me wanted to be left alone in my own little lonely rut—it was safe and predictable there. "I don't need anyone else," I told myself. "I'm doing just fine on my own!"

But she was always there, with an uplifting Scripture or a kind word. Gradually, my resistance wore down. I began to see that I needed to talk, to express many of the feelings I had kept bottled up inside for so long. To my surprise, we found we had many of the same feelings in common. Over the years, we have laughed, cried and celebrated together. She is now one of my dearest friends.

God taught me many things during that time. I learned that He wants us to live lives that are actively concerned with the feelings and welfare of others. I was surprised to discover that my shyness was often just selfishness disguised. With Jesus living inside me, I have a sound mind. I need give no place to fear.

We need each other. There's no denying it. There are certain types of healings that can only take place through interaction with others.

I know, Lord, that the most perfect form of intimacy lies in my relationship with you. But help me to remember that I am not an island, that it is healthy to reach out and be open with others. Amen.

Take a moment to praise God and list friends in Christ:

The Same Old Wreath!

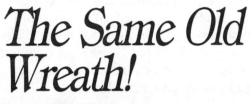

DAISY HEPBURN

During those celebration days each year you must explain to your children why you are celebrating—it is a celebration of what the Lord did for you when you left Egypt.
Exodus 13:8, TLB

Sliding to a stop at the intersection, the crunch of the icy snow under the tires reminded me that I had better keep my eyes on the road and hands securely on the steering wheel. But I couldn't help but take a peek at the wide green Christmas wreath apparently wired in place on the big stone chimney of the corner house.

It was well into January and I smiled at the sight of the wreath with its Merry Christmas message. Perhaps the lady of the house couldn't get it down in the midst of the Minnesota winter. I remembered that I still hadn't put all our decorations away, either, but at least they weren't outside, being advertised to the entire neighborhood.

A couple of weeks later, at the same intersection, I looked up and saw the same wreath, but this time with a different sign on it. A red heart hanging from the red ribbon announced: Happy Valentine's Day!

In March, it became a St. Patrick's Day wreath.

In April, the yellow ribbon read, This is a Happy Easter Wreath!

Then, in May, believe it or not, Happy Memorial Day!

By the Fourth of July, it was just a ring of brown twigs hanging on for dear life. I stopped the car in front of the house and finally dared to march up and ring the doorbell. No one was home. Perhaps it was better that way, but I did so want to meet the person who celebrated all year long—and always with a reason!

The Israelites were told by Moses to celebrate what God had done for them as they had observed God's laws and obeyed His instructions to protect their homes and families from the scourge of the death angel. They were to celebrate the Passover annually and be able to tell their children why they were celebrating.

Why do we go to church? Why do we worship God? To celebrate, of course! To celebrate what God has done for us—He has brought us out with great power. Do we take the time to explain that to our children?

Lord, help me to remember to hang a wreath on the chimney—and to explain to my children why we are celebrating. Amen.

Counting the Cost

ELIZABETH LARSON

They received the word with all readiness of mind, and searched the scriptures daily, whether those things were so.
Acts 17:11, *KJV*

e have many Bibles in our home, but one in particular is my sentimental favorite. It belonged to my husband before I adopted it, which makes it all the more dear to me. It has all his favorite passages underlined, his many little notes in the margins (I've read each one), and innumerable creases, smudges and torn spots, which are inevitable when a book is subjected to prolonged, loving abuse.

I must confess, I have added some features of my own: a few scribbles, various folds to mark my spot when I stop reading, the footprints of my preschooler who trampled the poor old book when I threw it behind the front seat of my car. But, worst of all, the cover is now threatening to fall off, due to the fact that I literally drop everything when my attention is caught by something else.

My favorite Bible. Its worth to me is great, but it wasn't until a few months ago that I realized the true cost of that book—a cost paid by others that I might freely possess my beloved book.

I was studying a history book when I came across a paragraph noting the words of a fifteenth-century bishop of England who wrote scornfully of certain women "which make themselves so wise by the Bible." It was the opinion of this bishop that women should have no right to study the Word of God. As I continued to read, I learned that some of the women so ridiculed by this bishop were wives and mothers who eventually died at the stake for refusing to accept any beliefs as God's truth "save what they can find expressly in the Bible."

I turned to my old favorite then, seeing it afresh. This book, which I handle with such careless, casual ease and freedom, would not be mine if it were not for those women (and men) who boldly claimed their right to have the Word of God—a right they paid for with their own blood.

Let me never forget, O Lord, the true cost and infinite value of your precious Word. Amen.

. . . Support and Encouragement

You Won't Fall

KATHY COLLARD MILLER

Now accept the one who is weak in faith.
Romans 14:1, *NASB*

Jeff, I won't let you fall!" I insisted, as I attempted to hold the swaying bike upright.

"Oh yes, I am! I'm going to fall!" my eight-year-old son cried out.

My patience wore thin as the hot sun beat down on us. "I told you, I'm holding you up! Start pedaling fast!"

Neighborhood friends on their bikes rode quickly past Jeff, urging him on. "Look, Jeff, do it this way!" But Jeff leaned the wrong way, fearful of crashing to the ground.

A few minutes later, I gave up. "Honey, we'll try again tomorrow. Don't worry, you'll learn."

That evening I talked with a friend about Jeff's struggle. She asked, "Have you tried to teach him someplace else so that he's not in front of his friends? Maybe he's afraid they'll see him fail."

The following Sunday evening, I loaded Jeff and his bike into the Blazer and drove to a distant school.

"Now, Jeff, there's no one around. We'll try it here."

Jeff tried to cooperate but our efforts seemed the same as before. Fifteen minutes later, though, Jeff unexpectedly stayed up by himself for a few seconds. "You did it!" I cheered.

By this time, a few children had arrived to play, and I could tell Jeff was watching to see whether they would make fun of him. I encouraged him to keep trying regardless of what they said or thought.

We continued our efforts but, becoming exhausted, we stopped and returned the next evening. Within 10 minutes, Jeff progressed to staying up 20 seconds, then longer, until, finally, he wobbly circled the playground again and again, a big grin on his face.

When we arrived home, Jeff breezed down the street on his bike, joyfully showing off his new accomplishment.

As I watched him, I couldn't help but think how the fear of failure or rejection prevents me from expressing my needs to other Christians. When I'm struggling with an area that eludes victory, I don't want people to see I'm not perfect, so I don't tell them of my struggle.

The wonderful truth, however, is that my brothers and sisters in Christ want to help me with prayer support and encouragement. They're just waiting for me to tell them what I need.

Lord, help me to see the encouragement that others want to give me. Amen.

. . . Finding Courage in Love

Have No Fear

HENRIETTA MEARS

There is no fear in love. But perfect love drives out fear. 1 John 4:18, *NIV*

One day in the mountain region of Scotland, a gigantic eagle snatched a little baby out of his crib and flew away with him. The people of the village ran out after the big bird, but the eagle perched itself upon a nearby mountain crag. Could the child possibly be rescued? A sailor tried to climb the ascent, but he was at last obliged to give up the attempt. A robust Highlander, accustomed to climbing those mountains, tried next and even his strength failed. At last a poor peasant woman came forward. She put her feet upon one shelf on the rock, then on the second, then on the third and in this manner she rose to the very top of the cliff. While all below held their breath for sheer fright, she came down step by step until she stood at the bottom of the rock with the child safely in her arms. Immediately shouts of praise arose from the crowd that had gathered.

Why did that woman succeed when the strong sailor and the experienced mountain climber had failed? Because that woman was the mother of the baby. Her love for her baby had given her the courage to do what the others had failed to do.

If the love of Christ is in your heart, you, too, will find that you will have the courage to do whatever He directs you to do.

Father, open our hearts to your perfect love that our fears may be dispelled. Amen.

Take a moment to praise God and list times you've found courage in His love:

Take

A

MOMENT

A

DAY

to learn about God . . .

. . . Through His Creation
We Learn About . . .

Heavenly Cheerleaders

MARY LOU CARNEY

*Wherefore seeing we also are compassed about
with so great a cloud of witnesses . . . let us
run with patience the race that is set before us.*
Hebrews 12:1, *KJV*

In the center of Camp Tecumseh, our
local YMCA camp, stands Mount Wood. This impos-
ing wooden structure is covered with slanted blocks.
By climbing up its sides, using the blocks for hand
and footholds, you can simulate rock climbing and
even duplicate the climbs performed on famous
mountains.

When I picked up my son from camp last summer, he persuaded me to try climbing Mount Wood.
The counselor strapped me into the safety harness
and buckled on my yellow helmet. "Don't worry," she
smiled. "You can't fall. We've got you if you slip."

As I began the climb, slanted wooden corners dug

into my palms. Soon, sweat soaked my forehead. It felt as though two-ton weights hung from my armpits. I was ready to give up when I heard the shouts from below. "Come on!" "You can do it!" "Almost there!" And somehow my throbbing calves found the strength to keep climbing.

It's that way with being a Christian, too. The climb is tough—and long. Sometimes you feel like giving up. Whenever that happens, look up. There's a great cloud of witnesses cheering you on—people like Abraham, Moses, Paul. Their encouragement will be just the boost you need to keep climbing.

Let us listen with our hearts, Lord, to the encouraging words of our heavenly cheering section. Amen.

———

Take a moment to praise God and list encouragers in your faith:

Slow Me Down, Lord

SUSAN F. TITUS

Be still, and know that I am God.
Psalm 46:10, *NIV*

I watched the waves roll into shore, breaking a few feet from my sand chair. At last, I had captured some time for myself! I dug my toes into the warm sand and breathed the cool ocean air.

My son caught a wave and rode it into shore. He smiled at me as he darted back into the surf, grasping his body board tightly under his arm.

I thought of how I had almost canceled this day at the beach. Working part-time, volunteering for church activities, and being a full-time wife and mother left me frazzled. I rushed from one activity to another, never feeling a sense of accomplishment.

Was I always too busy *doing* to take time to enjoy God's gifts to me?

My son and his friends straddled their boards, bobbing up and down in the water. A large wave crested, crashing over my son's shoulders. Everyone laughed. These children knew how to relax. They weren't rushed and tense.

Perhaps I crammed too much into my schedule. How could I know God's will for my life when I wasn't taking time to be in touch with my own feelings? I bowed my head and said a silent prayer, asking God to slow me down.

Raising my eyes to the horizon, I watched another wave surge into shore. A sense of God's peace rolled in with it and enveloped me. The tension in my neck and back muscles vanished. For the first time in months, I stopped worrying about all the undone chores at home. I concentrated on the present moment. I experienced the mystery and wonder of God's creation, the ocean.

God's voice is often a whisper. We must slow down and be silent to hear Him speak to us. Only then can He show us His will for each moment of our lives.

Dear Lord, help me to pause and listen to your voice. Allow the words to fill me with your peace and teach me your will for my life. Amen.

A Lovely Perfume

RUTH M. BATHAUER

Thanks be to God who leads us, wherever we are, on his own triumphant way and makes our knowledge of him spread throughout the world like a lovely perfume!
2 Corinthians 2:14, Phillips

erfumes — exotic, exciting — the perfect gift from that special someone. What woman doesn't respond to a new enticing fragrance? Recently, a movie star put her new perfume on the market, for which she was reportedly paid 2 million dollars. The more exotic, the more expensive it is.

The apostle Paul speaks of another perfume. Those of us who know Christ spread the knowledge of Him *throughout the world like a lovely perfume.*

Paul's thought is based on a graphic figure familiar to believers in his day. When a Roman general returned home victorious after a battle, a holiday was declared. Crowds gathered to applaud the victor as he led his captives, bound in chains, through the streets. A heavy scent from garlands of flowers and incense filled the air as the triumphant procession marched into the city.

The bottom line of this verse is victory. Christ is our victorious leader. The fragrance is our knowledge of Christ. As His love and power radiate through our lives, we become a sweet scent. Not because of what we have done, but because Christ lives within and we live in Him. We are filled by Him and are the medium by which the perfume of the saving knowledge of Christ is spread.

Daily we are bombarded with the sights and sounds of this world. We need to be tuned in to the Word of God so that we might hear His voice and allow Him to fill us so that we radiate not a stale, but a fresh, sweet scent of His presence in our lives.

Lord, thank you for your love. Teach us to give ourselves completely to you so that the fragrance of your presence may radiate from us. Amen.

Wounds of Death

CHRISTINE RICH

Then he said to Thomas, "Put your finger here; see my hands. Reach out your hand and put it into my side. Stop doubting and believe."
John 20:27, *NIV*

Am I a *doubting Thomas?* I would have insisted I wasn't before the death of my 12-year-old son, Bobby. But after the final grains of dirt had settled on my son's grave, doubts about God and His love began gnawing at the roots of my faith.

Two months after Bobby's death, my husband and I tried to escape our personal hell by taking a motorcycle trip from California to North Carolina.

The Nevada desert's vast horizon carried my thoughts back to fiery orange and yellow sunsets seen on numerous camping trips with Bobby. Tears burned my swollen, red eyes—eyes that could see only emptiness and despair. Everything had died with my son. I felt stripped of my very being.

"God," I cried, "where are you?"

Crossing familiar territory seemed to drive my pain deeper. Everywhere I looked were memories of happy vacations spent with our son.

As we approached the state of Colorado, a strange feeling crept over me. Then, like a bolt of lightning, it struck. "Colorado," I whispered slowly. "We've never been to Colorado with Bobby. No memories here!"

Anxiously, I craned my neck around my husband to get a glimpse of the upcoming border marker. The word *freedom* pulsated through my veins.

In the distance, I could see a sign. As we got closer, I yelled, "There it is! Colorado!"

Fixing my eyes upon the sign, I watched it as we zipped by. Crossing the state line was more than entering new territory for me; it was the turning point in my grieving. Through the beauty of Colorado, I began to see that God still cared for me and that He had never left my side.

As we climbed up to the Colorado high country with its brilliant green meadows sprinkled with brightly colored wild flowers, I raised my eyes toward the majestic blue sky. For the first time since Bobby's death, I thanked God for filling my soul with His peace, and my body with His strength.

Like the apostle Thomas, I had to have proof that God was real. I had experienced the wounds brought by death, and God had helped me see that my wounds, like the wounds of Jesus, would one day be scars for living through believing and trusting in Him.

Dear heavenly Father, when my doubting-Thomas ways begin to surface, fill my soul with your peace and my body with your strength. Amen.

. . . Purity and Growth

The Gardener

ELOISE BUSHA

And their soul shall be as a watered garden.
Jeremiah 31:12, *KJV*

A gardener I'm not. An owner of a flower garden I am. Therefore, in order to enjoy my flowers, I have to make a choice: I can hire someone to care for them, which would be silly, since my flower garden is very small; or I can learn to care for them myself, which I am trying to do.

So far, my flower gardening has constituted a minimum of procedures. First, I prepare the soil by spading, raking and picking out stones. Second, I buy the plants. Third, I plant them. Fourth, I water them. And fifth, I wait for Mother Nature to do her work.

During the waiting period, I am amazed to see, however, that my potentially beautiful plants are not thriving and blooming in abundance. Rather, in their place is a strange conglomeration of green shoots of various sizes and arrangements. These green strangers I soon learn are weeds.

Thus begins another procedure—weeding the flower beds. This, as every gardener can verify, is a never-ending process.

As the summer passes, I experience contrasting emotions, such as elation when I behold colorful blossoms adorning my greenery, and frustration when I realize that, unless I spend another hour on my knees weeding, the weeds will soon take over.

As I think about this, I realize how like a flower garden our lives are. God has placed us on this earth in order to add something of value. Our lives are to bloom and show forth the beauty of His love and mercy.

With proper nurturing of godly attributes and with constant weeding of unsuitable actions and characteristics unbecoming to our witness, we will become the people God intends us to be.

Sometimes our heavenly Father weeds out of our lives things like envy, jealousy, pride, bitterness. God's Holy Word and His Spirit are the tools He uses to accomplish His gardening.

It's when the Spirit takes me to my knees in prayer that I know God is at work in me perfecting His plan for my life.

Thank you, Father, for showing me that you care enough to weed out my faults. Help me to be willing to spend time on my knees so you can continue your work in me. Amen.

A Case of Puppy Love

ELIZABETH LARSON

But I say unto you, Love your enemies.
Matthew 5:44, *KJV*

It wasn't until our second year of marriage that I realized my sweet, lovable, wonderful husband did indeed have a serious fault—he likes dogs. Now, don't get me wrong. I like dogs, too—as long as they are owned, fed and restrained by someone else.

To be perfectly honest, I am terrified of dogs. So, when Jerry announced that he had bought a dog, I nearly collapsed.

"Sweetheart, it's only a puppy," Jerry pleaded, giving me his most soulful *Mom-can-I-keep-him* look.

"Puppy!" I cried, backing away from our new Malamute. "That's no puppy, that's a horse!"

247

"You'll get used to him," Jerry assured me, determined to have his beloved pet.

Equally determined, I launched a campaign against Puppy, silently declaring him the enemy. At first, Puppy reciprocated, seeming to recognize me as his adversary. He stole my dustpans, towels, shoes, gloves, and my son's toys, chewing them all to pulp before discarding them in some spot where I would be sure to find their remains. He howled, chased the neighbor's cattle—provoking deserved complaints—and then ignored me when I tried to correct him.

That was our first year together. Since then, Puppy has matured considerably. In his new adult dignity, he has changed his strategy. To my astonishment, he now greets me joyously, lick-kissing my fingers, then ignoring my scowls while he parades about the yard, jauntily waving the plume of his tail at me. And, whenever I have to feed him, he gazes at me adoringly before he eats. In addition, he serves as an uninvited escort when I walk down our country road, protectively keeping all other dogs at a distance.

In short, he is loving me into a humbling truce. And that, I suppose, was what God had in mind when He allowed the "enemy" to infiltrate my life in the form of a very large, very lovable dog. I still have a lot to learn about loving my enemies, but I've made a lot of progress since Jerry brought Puppy home to live with us.

Puppy is winning. But don't tell Jerry.

Dear Lord, help me to see my enemies—even (shudder) dogs—as your beloved creatures. Amen.

In Pleasant Places

KATHI MILLS

The boundary lines have fallen for me in pleasant places; surely I have a delightful inheritance. Psalm 16:6, *NIV*

The sun was warm on my back as I stood watering the lawn, the spray from the hose drifting back at me on the breeze. As I closed my eyes and listened to the birds in the peach tree overhead, the words of Psalm 16 whispered gently to my troubled heart.

Where was David, I wondered, when he was able to proclaim that? Was everything going well in his life? Or was he able to say this in the midst of chaos and tragedy?

Because that's where I was that morning. In the midst of trials that threatened to overwhelm me. My father-in-law had recently passed away, and now my father had just had a heart attack. I wanted desperately to contact my brother Bob, to tell him what was going on in our family, to tell him to come home—but I couldn't. Bob, who had been so instrumental in leading many in our family to know the Lord, had disappeared almost a year earlier. I had no idea where he was—or even how he was.

I recoiled the hose and sank to my knees in the warm, moist earth of the flower bed, tugging at the unruly weeds that mockingly assured me of their return. Oh, David, I cried silently, were those great words spoken by you on your coronation day? Or were you, like me, in Ziklag, devastated, discouraged, despairing?

Somehow I'd like to believe that it was at Ziklag, or a time like that, when David penned that great psalm. At Ziklag, where he returned with his men to find that the enemy had invaded and burned the city in his absence, taking the women and children captive. At Ziklag, where his own men turned against him, blaming him for the disaster that had befallen them, threatening to stone him. At Ziklag, where, in the midst of it all, the Bible says, "David found strength in the Lord his God" (1 Sam. 30:6, *NIV*).

Standing up and brushing the dirt from my hands and knees, I looked around me at my home, my garden, the street where my friends and neighbors lived. I wiped my forehead with my sleeve and went inside, walking through the cool darkness from room to room, remembering the laughter, the tears, the triumphs.

And suddenly I knew it didn't matter where I was, or what the circumstances were. Like David, I could strengthen myself in God and say with confidence,

"The boundary lines have fallen for me in pleasant places; surely I have a delightful inheritance."

Father, help us to look beyond our trials and our circumstances, and to appreciate our heavenly heritage. Amen.

Morning Glory
KATHI MILLS

As morning spread upon the mountains
I beheld the shining of His glory;
rays of expectation diffused
    through a holy spectrum,
dancing and shimmering
    with delight.

The Autumn of My Years

MARY BECKWITH

They are like trees along a river bank bearing luscious fruit each season without fail. Their leaves shall never wither, and all they do shall prosper. Psalm 1:3, *TLB*

The Michigan trees waved their bright orange and red leaves at me as we cruised the expressway on our last trip back home.

I love mid-West falls—the warm autumn breezes, the beautifully painted leaves signaling another summer's end. As a child, I remember kicking through piles of maple and elm leaves, then we'd rake them up again and have a big bonfire. Mmm, the smell of burning leaves!

Autumn. The signal of the end of one season— and the beginning of another. In a way, that's how I feel right now. For life has its seasons too. And I feel as if I'm in the autumn of my years.

My summertime is fading quickly, as I watch my children, one by one, leave the nest; and the supple body of my youth rapidly changing form—and not for the better.

But, you know, I really don't mind what's taking place, now that I've accepted the thought of getting older and I've begun to realize the harvest of earlier seasons.

For one thing, I'm able to pursue my career full time, not to mention having more time to myself. My husband and I can come and go as we please, even spend weekends away together. And, now and then, I'm even revered by some as having a little wisdom!

I have time to spend with my Lord in prayer and delve into His Word. I can fellowship with my friends, knowing I'm not taking away from my family. Autumn. It's a lovely time of life.

But autumn leaves wither and fall. The beautiful reds and oranges of fall turn to brown. Warm breezes turn frigid. Gray skies signal snow is on the way. Winter approaches.

My season of winter will come too. When it does, will my leaves wither and fall? Will the color of excitement for what God has done for me turn brown? Will the warmth I now feel for others cool, my joy turn gray with boredom, until at last I am frigid and not enjoyable to be around? Will my zeal to share the good news fade until I am no longer producing fruit for my King?

God willing, I pray not. For I choose to claim God's promise that each of us who delight in the law of the Lord and meditate on His Word will be like a tree firmly planted by streams of water, which yields its fruit in its season, and its leaf does not wither.

Thank you, Lord, for your promise that my leaves will never wither, that as long as I love you and meditate on your Word, I will remain firmly planted and I will yield fruit in all my seasons. Amen.

Look to the Trees
DIANTHA AIN

Know the power of thyself
By looking at the trees
Reaching skyward to their God
Responding to each breeze
Giving rest to wayward birds
A home for some to nest
A haven safe for fledglings
'Til they can meet the test

Shapes determined through the years
By storms that stress their cores
Beauty stunted by a drought
Or parasitic bores
Broken branches clinging
Black trunks seared by fire
Always there's a quiet strength
To which I would aspire

The secret gift of living well
Is known to every tree
Why then is it so hard for us
To simply learn to be

The Silence

GLORIA GAITHER

Be still, and know that I am God.
Psalm 46:10, *KJV*

Stillness is more audible than any sound, not tinny like so many sounds I hear these days.

The silence is full and rich, insistent . . . demanding that I listen and suggesting always that I'd be foolish not to. Only fools refuse the counsel of the wise, and this silence seems to know everything. It seems I've been a prodigal, traipsing along behind the band just like a thoughtless gypsy anywhere the living was easy, stealing morsels when I could have had the loaf.

Maybe it's the oaks and beeches. These oaks have housed a thousand generations of owls and jays, and have withstood abuse from countless woodpeckers and men. They've seen the fleet-footed native children tossing pebbles at their roots and chasing little fawns around between them. They've stood and heard the council casting lots for war or peace while fragrant pipe smoke wafted through their branches.

Perhaps it is the brook, whispering of its secret travels, nurturing the earth along its way, or maybe it's the earth, the pregnant fertile earth, pulling me like influential kin back to my moorings and my heritage.

The earth is calling me home to the simple and eternal things. It persistently calls me to reject the glitter of the transient and return to Father's house.

The silence—a voice asking one pointed and unavoidable question: Will I return and inherit the earth? And here in the silence, the only sound to be heard is the whisper of my own answer.

Father, teach us to be silent that we might hear your heartbeat in the midst of a noisy world. Amen.

From *Let's Make a Memory,* by Gloria Gaither and Shirley Dobson, copyright 1983; used by permission of Word Books, publisher, Waco, Texas.

Heaven Will Be Like That

JONI EARECKSON TADA

He will wipe every tear from their eyes. There will be no more death or mourning or crying or pain, for the old order of things has passed away. Revelation 21:4, *NIV*

When I think of heaven, I think of a time when I will be welcomed home. I remember when I was on my feet what a cozy, wonderful feeling it was to come home after hockey practice. How pleasant to hear the familiar clanging of bells against our back door as I swung it open. Inside awaited the sights, sounds, and smells of warmth and love. Mom would greet me with a wide smile as she dished out food into big bowls ready to be set on the table. I'd throw down my sweat suit and hockey stick, bound into the den, and greet Daddy. He'd turn from his desk, taking off his glasses, then he'd give me a big "hi" and ask me how practice was.

For Christians, heaven will be like that. We will see old friends and family who have gone on before us. Our kind heavenly Father will greet us with open, loving arms. Jesus, our older brother, will be there to welcome us, too. We won't feel strange or insecure. We will feel like we're home . . . for we *will* be home. Jesus said it was a place prepared for us.

We'll have new bodies and new minds! I myself will be able to run to friends and embrace them for the first time. I will lift my new hands before the hierarchy of heaven—shouting to everyone within earshot, "Worthy is the Lamb who was slain to receive blessing and honor. For He freed my soul from the clutches of sin and death, and now He has freed my body as well!"

The wrongs and injustices of earth will be righted. God will measure out our tears which He has kept in His bottle, and not a single one will go unnoticed. He who holds all reasons in His hand will give us the key that makes sense out of our most senseless sufferings. And that's only the beginning.

Thank you, Father, for the beautiful promise of heaven. Amen.

Taken from *A Step Further* by Joni Eareckson and Steve Estes. Copyright 1978 by Joni Eareckson and Steve Estes. Used by permission of Zondervan Publishing House.

... The Cleansing of Tears

Jesus Wept

FAY ANGUS

Let your tears run down like a river.
Lamentations 2:18, *NASB*

Our body needs our tears as much as our emotions need to have them flow. They lubricate our eyes and keep them moist; they cleanse and lift a piece of lint or speck of dust; they wash away the fumes that smart and irritate.

Within each of us are reservoirs brimful with tears.

Tears of joy and gratitude. Sentimental tears that well up when our hearts are touched—a petal hung with dew, the soft curve of a baby's cheek, or weepy, inexplicable tears that flow with a lovely piece of music.

Tears of frustration and anger. Tears of disappointment and hurt. Tears of regret. Then the sobbing, choking tears of grief.

Thank God for men strong enough to cry.

One man said, "Sometimes it's just not enough to shake another man's hand firmly, look him in the eye, and nod. Sometimes it's not enough to put your arm around a woman, and pat her gently on the back while she cries for both of you."

Jesus wept—thank God.

Dear Father, thank you for the cleansing power of tears. And thank you for the example of your Son who was a Man strong enough to cry. Amen.

Taken from *How to Do Everything Right and Live to Regret It* by Fay Angus. © Copyright 1983 by Fay Angus. Published by Harper & Row. Used by permission.

Take a moment to praise God and list times when your tears have brought healing:

... The Stillness of His Love

Plenty of Nothin'

RUTH BELL GRAHAM

The whole earth is at rest, and is quiet: they break forth into singing. Isaiah 14:7, *KJV*

Evening was creeping along the valleys and up the ridges. The breeze rustling leaves in the treetops had stilled. Not even the chatter of a katydid broke the silence.

I was rocking quietly on the front porch when our six-year-old burst through the screen door, letting it slam behind him. He settled noisily into the rocker next to mine and whispered, "Shhh. Be quiet, Mom. Don't make any noise . . . and you will hear plenty of nuffin."

So we shushed, were quiet, didn't make any noise, and heard plenty of nothing. Finally I whispered, "Do you like hearing nothing?"

"No," he replied. "I like noise!" With that, he bounded out of the rocker and jerked open the screen door. Darting inside, he let it slam behind him.

Me? I like "plenty of nothin'." It's the noise of civilization that disturbs and grates. Nature's noises, I have discovered, refresh and relax me.

The rustle of the wind in the tops of the trees or the roar of it across the ridge behind the house. The chirping of a cricket or the orchestration of katydids from midsummer until frost. The full moon rising, huge and silent, over Little Rainbow Ridge. The expectant stillness . . . .

On such evenings, Bill and I will sit together on the front porch when he is home, quietly talking, or, when words are not needed, just listening to "plenty of nothin'."

And along with the deepening shadows in the valleys below, the darting of the evening's first bat across the darkening sky, come the memories . . . .

Dear God, thank you for quiet times and your creation and the time to enjoy them both. Amen.

Adapted from *It's My Turn* by Ruth Bell Graham, copyright © 1982 by Ruth Bell Graham (Old Tappan, NJ: Fleming H. Revell Company; London: Hodder & Stoughton Ltd). Used by permission.

Postscript
... A Promise for Tomorrow

NO MORE GREY
by Jill Briscoe

No more grey, Lord;
colors crowd my life,
soft colors of love.
No more sterile air;
fresh winds blow through my mind.
See my thoughts now,
falling into line like
rows of orderly soldiers,
marching merrily to war,
sure of victory,
fighting for a cause.
No more empty spaces to live in;
Jesus is here.
Sweet friend,
determined to make me His confidant.
No more grey, Lord;
colors crowd my life,
soft colors of love.

Meet Our Contributors

DIANTHA AIN has touched the lives of more than 6,000 children with "Cultivating Creativity in Children" workshops. She has received numerous poetry and music awards and has published a book of poems and drawings. She resides in Simi Valley, California.

LINDA ALEAHMAD is editor for *Winning Edge*, a publication for businesswomen, and former fiction editor for *Today* magazine. In addition to editing and writing, she and her husband, Iradg, have their own business. They have two children and reside in Simi Valley, California.

FAY ANGUS, because of her particular blend of faith and humor, has been called the evangelical Erma Bombeck. She is an author, and popular speaker for conventions and women's groups. She lives in Sierra Madre, California with her husband and two children.

MARLENE ASKLAND, a ventriloquist, has taught Sunday School for 34 years. She enjoys calligraphy and decoupage, painting and gardening. Her husband of 30 years is a pastor; they have four grown children and live in Woodland, Washington.

ETHEL BARRETT is one of America's most inspirational Christian personalities. A popular conference speaker, she is especially loved for her gift of story-telling. She has authored over 40 books and makes her home in California.

RUTH M. BATHAUER is managing editor for Regal Books. She is currently writing her second course for the Joy of Living Bible Studies and has written numerous articles for denominational magazines. She resides in Ventura, California.

CAROL BECKERDITE is an interior decorator, wife and mother of two children. She is active in her local chapter of Women's Aglow and has written for numerous Christian newspapers and publications. She makes her home in Santa Paula, California.

MARY BECKWITH is an editor for Regal Books. She has written and conducted a variety of workshops for women, young girls and, most recently, writers. She enjoys traveling, organizing, teaching and correspondence. She and her husband, Clint, reside in Ventura, California with their three children.

JANET CHESTER BLY has written more than 200 articles, short stories and poems for a variety of Christian publications. She has also written nine books with her husband, Stephen Bly, six of which are part of the Crystal Series. The Blys have three children and reside in Fillmore, California.

MARTHA BOLTON, author of four books of comedy sketches and monologues, has won numerous awards for script writing and is a staff writer for comedian Bob Hope. In addition, she has written many articles and humorous poems. She resides in Simi

Valley, California with her husband, Russ, and three sons.

JILL BRISCOE is author of several books, many of which were written with her husband, Stuart Briscoe. Jill has an active writing and speaking ministry and is coordinator of Women's Ministries at Elmbrook Church in Waukesha, Wisconsin. The Briscoes have three children and one grandchild.

MARGARET BROWNLEY is interested in anything that can be turned into an article or story and has written two novels and numerous articles to prove it. She teaches novel writing and has received numerous state and national writing awards. Her family resides in Simi Valley, California.

ELOISE BUSHA published her own devotional and has written numerous poems and articles. She enjoys teaching Sunday School and Bible studies and has presented seminars and music workshops for women. Mother of six children, she and her husband, Don, make their home in Genesee, Michigan.

MARY LOU CARNEY is an award-winning poet, author and speaker. A former teacher, she has published nine books and written numerous poems and articles. She is listed in Outstanding Young Women and Who's Who in American Poets. Her family resides in Chesterton, Indiana.

ELAINE WRIGHT COLVIN is a writer, poet and consultant. In addition to addressing writers' conferences, clubs and creative writing classes nationwide, she organizes and directs five national Christian Writers' Conferences. Her family resides on Bainbridge Island, Washington.

BARBARA COOK is an author, speaker, musician and ordained minister. Her ministry to women, A Touch of Beauty, included a syndicated daily radio program and Bible studies. She and husband, Jerry, address pastors' conferences and marriage seminars. The Cooks make their home in Kirkland, Washington.

DONNA FLETCHER CROW has written 2 films, 7 plays and nearly 20 books. Her writing has appeared in numerous publications and she has received several writing awards. She is a conference speaker and teaches a variety of workshops. Her family resides in Boise, Idaho.

JUNE CURTIS is a singer, writer, speaker and has traveled worldwide on several lay-missionary projects. She has ministered with Christian Women's Clubs and Councils for nearly 20 years. She is a regular contributor to *Virtue* Magazine. Her family lives in Eugene, Oregon.

SHIRLEY DOBSON is an author, a wife, mother and homemaker. She has served as leader in Bible Study Fellowship and as director of women's ministries for her church. She has appeared on many radio and TV shows with her husband Dr. James Dobson. The Dobsons reside in Southern California.

GLORIA GAITHER is author, speaker, teacher, lyricist, recording artist and performer. She has authored five books and numerous articles. She has been principal lyricist for more than 350 songs with her husband Bill Gaither. The Gaithers live in Indiana.

RUTH BELL GRAHAM, wife of evangelist Billy Graham, is the author of three books. The Grahams have five children and fifteen grandchildren and make their home in Montreat, North Carolina.

MARIETTA GRAMCKOW is a wife, mother, grandmother and great-grandmother. She enjoys reading, sewing and crocheting, and has a letter-writing ministry. With her husband of 40 years, Hans, she resides in LaCenter, Washington.

DORIS GREIG is the mother of four grown children. She is founder, author and leader for the Joy of Living Bible Studies, an evangelical and nondenominational program for individual, church and home study. She has authored one book. She and her husband Bill live in Ventura, California.

BERYL HENNE enjoys reading, music and crocheting. She has been editor of a children's magazine and has taught writers' workshops. Beryl makes her home in Delta, British Columbia with her husband and daughter.

DAISY HEPBURN is a conference and retreat speaker, and author of four books and eight Bible study booklets. She is founder and director of The Hope of Our

Heritage women's conferences. She and her husband of 36 years have 2 children and reside in San Francisco.

NICOLE HILL is a former college instructor with her Master's in business administration. She has won awards for her poetry, enjoys Bible study, art, music, government, cooking and interior decorating. She and her husband, Terry, have two daughters and make their home in Simi Valley, California.

MARILYN HOCHHEISER, an award-winning poet, teaches creative writing workshops and poetry classes. She enjoys gardening, stage plays, evangelism and has originated poetry readings for poetry-lovers. She has three grown children and along with her husband, Sid, resides in Simi Valley, California.

DIANE JUSTUS enjoys writing, reading, walking, aerobics and working with children. She teaches a junior high girls' Sunday School class and a women's Bible study for young moms and wives. Diane and her husband, Steve, have three children and reside in Clinton, Washington.

BERIT KJOS has written a series of Bible studies and enjoys hiking, cross-country skiing and singing. She and her husband, Andy, have three sons and make their home in Los Altos Hills, California.

ELIZABETH LARSON is a pen name for Kacy Gramckow, who has just completed her first novel. She enjoys reading—everything!—needlepoint, cooking and, of course, writing. She and her husband, Jerry, have one son. They live in LaCenter, Washington.

SHARON MAHOE enjoys piano, choir, painting, reading, antique stores, old books and music. She edits a newsletter and enjoys one-on-one fellowship with friends, and taking long bike rides. She makes her home in San Diego, California.

HENRIETTA MEARS was "Teacher" to her beloved Sunday School classes, and untold thousands were touched by her life beginning in the 1920s and up until her death in 1963. In 1933 she founded Gospel Light Publications and subsequent to that Forest Home Christian Conference Center.

KATHY COLLARD MILLER is the author of two books and numerous articles. She is a speaker and teaches seminars based on her books. Listed in Who's Who of U.S. Editors, Poets, and Authors, Kathy and her husband Larry have two children and live in Placentia, California.

KATHI MILLS is an award-winning writer who lives in Santa Paula, California with her husband, Larry, and the youngest of her three sons. Listed in *Who's Who of Writers and Authors,* Kathi is under contract for three more books scheduled for release in 1989.

LINDA MONTOYA has published in *Guideposts* and *Working Mother* magazines. She has received many awards in public speaking and was area graduate

271

supervisor for Bible Study Fellowship for several years. She and her husband, Frank, have three daughters and reside in Ventura, California.

EUGENIA PRICE is the author of 35 books, which have sold over 16 million copies and have been translated into 16 languages. She also had a popular radio series and an extensive speaking career. Considered a major writer in the Christian field, Eugenia Price makes her home on St. Simon's Island, off the coast of Georgia.

PEG RANKIN has written two books and a third with her husband, Lee. She is a popular conference speaker, and together the Rankins teach a variety of seminars and Bible studies. They also have a tape ministry. The Rankins have three married sons and live in Monmouth Beach, New Jersey.

DIANE REICHICK has written articles for a variety of local newspapers. She enjoys reading, oil painting, calligraphy, restoring furniture, gourmet cooking and gardening. She and her husband, Ron, have two children and reside in Simi Valley, California.

CHRISTINE RICH has published many feature articles about local personalities, and has been editor for two newsletters. She enjoys studying the craft of writing, oil painting and travel. She and her husband, Bob, have two children and make their home in Liberty, Missouri.

DALE EVANS ROGERS is an actress-singer, speaker and

writer. She travels nationwide, appearing on radio and television. She has her own television program and has authored over a dozen books. She and her husband, Roy Rogers, make their home in Apple Valley, California.

LENORE C. SCHUETZ has published articles and children's stories. She enjoys reading, co-ed softball, bowling and camping. She and her husband have two children and live in Simi Valley, California.

INGRID SHELTON has written several children's books, children's curriculum, and numerous stories and articles. She enjoys puppetry, reading and travel. In addition, she has taught writing workshops. Ingrid and her husband, Philip, have one daughter and live in Abbotsford, British Columbia.

ADREW ROGERS SLYDER enjoys writing and oil painting and is active with her local chamber of commerce. Adrew has two children and three grandchildren. She and her husband make their home in Simi Valley, California.

CAROL STEWART, a published writer, has a women's ministry where she hosts and teaches Bible studies. She enjoys reading, counted cross stitch, and her work with junior high learning and emotionally disabled students. She and husband, Ed, have two grown children and live in Hillsboro, Oregon.

LUCI SWINDOLL has written three books, is a popular conference speaker and has been on many radio and television programs. A long-time executive with Mobil Oil Corp., Luci recently became involved in her brother Chuck's ministry, Insight for Living, in Fullerton, California.

JONI EARECKSON TADA has been an inspiration to millions of people since her tragic accident, which left her a quadriplegic. She and her husband Ken live north of Los Angeles, where her ministry Joni and Friends is headquartered.

SUSAN F. TITUS is the author of two books, numerous children's stories and curriculum and is associate director for the Writers Institute at Biola University. Susan lives in Fullerton, California with her husband, Dick, and two teenage sons.

BONNIE WHEELER has written many books and articles and is a popular speaker for writers' conferences and women's groups. Her interests include time management studies, adoptions, the physically challenged and the family. The Wheelers have six children and live in Union City, California.

MARIAN WIGGINS is managing editor for children's curriculum at Gospel Light Publications. In addition to writing and editing, she has been a speech pathologist and speech-language specialist. She enjoys music, and makes her home in Ventura, California.

More Regal Books Written Especially for Today's Busy Woman. . .

Faith and Savvy Too!
The Christian Woman's Guide to Money—Judith Briles
A practical guide to money management for women. Topics include how to make money work in today's market, how to use credit wisely, how to make financial decisions and much more.   5419383

We Didn't Know They Were Angels:
Hospitality Even When It's Inconvenient—Doris W. Greig
Hospitality is a gift to others that should be nurtured. You don't need sterling silver or a gourmet kitchen; all you need is a willing spirit and an open door. Includes over 300 family-tested recipes.   5418802

Free to Be God's Woman: Building a
Solid Foundation for a Healthy Self-Image—Janet Congo
A book for the Christian woman who seeks a better understanding of herself and her relationships with those she loves.   5419407

I'd Speak Out on the Issues
If I Only Knew What to Say—Jane Chastain
This book explains, in a step-by-step format, what you can do to make your opinion heard. The most hotly contested issues of our day are covered including school-based health clinics, abortion, pornography and more.   5418968

Romancing Your Marriage—H. Norman Wright
Maintaining intimacy and romance in your marriage is possible and fun! Best-selling author Norm Wright shows spouses the benefits from learning to love your imperfect partner, ridding yourself of resentment and trying creative romantic suggestions.   5419168

LOOK FOR THESE AND OTHER EXCITING REGAL TITLES AT YOUR REGULAR CHRISTIAN BOOKSTORE!
OR CALL 1-(800)-235-3415   1-(800) 227-4025
Outside CA   Inside CA

#300